FAST FOOD SLOW DEATH

by
Peter Taylor

Fast Food Slow Death

Author: Peter Taylor

Copyright © 2024 Peter Taylor

The right of Peter Taylor to be identified as author of this work has been asserted by the author in accordance with section 77 and 78 of the Copyright, Designs and Patents Act 1988.

ISBN 978-1-83538-340-7 (Paperback)
      978-1-83538-341-4 (E-Book)

Cover Design and Book Layout by:
    White Magic Studios
    www.whitemagicstudios.co.uk

Published by:
    Maple Publishers
    Fairbourne Drive, Atterbury,
    Milton Keynes,
    MK10 9RG, UK
    www.maplepublishers.com

A CIP catalogue record for this title is available from the British Library.

All rights reserved. No part of this book may be reproduced or translated by any form or by any means, electronic or mechanical, including photocopying, recording or by any information storage and retrieval system without written permission from the author.

This book is a memoir. It reflects the author's recollections of experiences over time. Some names and characteristics have been changed, some events have been compressed, and some dialogues have been recreated, and the Publisher hereby disclaims any responsibility for them.

CONTENTS

Foreword 4

Introduction 7

Chapter 1 – The Human Cell 10

Chapter 2 – Acidity in the Diet 20

Chapter 3 – The Toxic Load 26

Chapter 4 – Macro Nutrients 31

Chapter 5 – Food Values 38

Chapter 6 – Vitamins and Minerals 44

Chapter 7 – Good Foods 66

Chapter 8 – Average Foods 94

Chapter 9 – Poor Foods 120

Chapter 10 – Food Production and Land Distribution 142

                Food Production – Land Use 147

Chapter 11 – Food Production – Farming Methods 149

Chapter 12 – Food Waste 154

Chapter 13 – Food Production and Health 158

Chapter 14 – Modified Food 166

Chapter 15 – Fast Food – the American Story 174

Chapter 16 – Food Production and Climate Change 178

Chapter 17 – Conclusion 185

Foreword

It is obvious that we have a serious problem with processed and ultra processed foods otherwise known as fast food.

The response from governments of relatively prosperous countries is the same. It is incumbent upon them to ensure food security and sufficient food for the poorest of their populations and therefore cheap food availability is essential. Another way of saying this is that 'we the government must ensure the poorest have access to the most highly processed foods available because it is the cheapest.'

Flip this over and translate it. 'We the government must support the fast food industry because it offers cheap, affordable food for our poorest citizens.' Which sounds laudable but for the omissions. Fast food is cheap because it is habit forming, ensuring that once a person 'gets a taste for it' it is hard to resist. Loyalty, if you like. It is high in calories, salt, sugar, fats and low in nutritional value. There is almost no fibre in it. It will lead to chronic conditions if consumed on a regular basis which is WHY it is habit forming to ensure that it IS consumed on a regular basis. It will lead to chronic conditions with diabetes and obesity heading the list. It will increase costs of health and social services so national productivity will be affected. It has a detrimental effect upon global warming due to the farming methods used to produce it. Apart from being cheap it is a very poor food option. It is cheap because it IS a very poor food option and governments are condemning poor people to consume it. This is the way I see it.

So What is the Solution?

A symbol coded system as demonstrated in the following chapters can and should be introduced on every food item, enabling people to judge which foods they wish to purchase based upon its overall nutritional value.

Wholesome food must be available to everyone and will therefore require subsidies. Since processed and highly processed food gives higher profits for less value it should be taxed. Sugar, salt, GM, plastic packaging, use of chemicals such as flavourings and colourings should all have a taxable penalty introduced gradually but, as in the tobacco industry, increased over time until it becomes just as profitable to produce whole food as it would have been to produce fast food. Mass whole food production instead of mass processed food production. The critical mass brings the price down. The taxable income to the government would not change. As the price of fast food goes up creating fewer consumers the tax income also goes up and as whole food prices come down tax income remains the same as more people consume it.

The results would eventually have a financial benefit for governments, producers and consumers in the end. Chronic illness would be reduced, health services would benefit from less pressure, productivity would increase as people would have fewer sick days, social services would spend less time on depressed people, more people would be involved in producing local produce, less meat would be consumed and the planet would benefit too from lower greenhouse gas emissions.

Why Isn't Enough Being Done?

The power of the relevant corporations, by lobbying governments and advertising to consumers, plus the employment of huge numbers of scientists and technical staff ensures the food industry remains in the grip of 'for profit only' and sometimes ruthless owners.

Governments are frightened that the moment they introduce higher taxes on any element of the fast food industry the media will accuse them of attacking the poor who cannot feed their families when in actual fact they are being fed poor quality food which damages their health and that of the planet. Governments need to recognise this and make their case for taxing fast food while subsidising whole food. A tiny bit of that exists but it is so tiny as to be practically invisible.

Introduction

Are you confused about what food is good for you and what is not? Are you tired of all the chatter about what is best for you? The number of diets, the dangers of eating the wrong food, the endless cookery Programmes which recommend you eat things you will never attempt in your kitchen? Do you even bother to cook? Or are you just too busy to even think about cooking good food, laying up the table for your children who only seem to graze on pizza or some form of fast food? Is the whole food issue just driving you to a 'couldn't care less' attitude? Well, you certainly are not alone and sometimes with good reason.

Few, if any of us, understand the details, that by law, the food industry is compelled to print on all their packaging. Which, let's be honest, is a waste of time.

Take this as an example

Chicken Sandwich

This is what we are told on the back of the package.

Total Energy per 100 gms – 157 calories.

Energy per pack – 281 calories

Protein per 100 gms – 11 gms

Protein per pack – 19.7 gms

Carbohydrate per 100 gms – 22 gms

Carbohydrate per pack – 39.5 gms

Fat per 100 gms – 2 gms

Fat per pack – 3.7 gms

Fibre per 100 gms – 3 gms

Fibre per pack – 5.3 gms

Salt per 100 gms – 0.20 gms

Salt per pack – 0.90 gms

Ingredients – Malted bread, Roast Chicken, Leaf Mix, Chive Mayonnaise, Cucumber, Tomato

Contains: - Wheat Flour, Malted Flakes, Bran, Gluten, Water, Yeast, Barley Malt, Salt, Vinegar, Rapeseed, Emulsifiers, Treatment agent, Chicken Breast, Cornflour, Free Range Egg, Milk Powder, Lemon Juice, Sugar, Mustard, Iceberg Lettuce, Apollo Lettuce.

Is all this good, bad or doesn't it matter? Do you know how much salt you should eat on a daily basis, or sugar, or fat, or anything for that matter? Would you spend time trying to extrapolate the information before deciding to buy one of these sandwiches? I doubt it. So what's the point of showing you? Do you know how much protein you should be consuming daily? If not, how can this information help you? The sandwich contains about 40 gms of carbohydrate. Is this good or not? Do you know that carbohydrates turn to sugar and that excess sugar turns to fat? Is 40 gms a lot? Fat: 2.1 gms ... how much fat are we allowed? Salt: 0.50 gms ... doesn't look like a lot. Fibre: 3 gms ... is this important?

None of this information is of any use unless we understand how much of anything we need and most of us do not, so what is the point of putting this information on the package? As it happens this sandwich is rather poor on nutritional value and frankly is not good value even if it tastes delicious, which it almost certainly will with the added flavours and colourings.

Once you have learned a little about how your body assimilates the food you eat and why it is necessary to understand what, in general, is good and not good to consume, you will understand why the simple code system which I have outlined is useful. Sadly, it doesn't exist in shops yet but with what you may learn in this book it will help you understand more about what values the food you buy contains.

As the book progresses you will learn about the fast food industry and draw your own conclusions about its impact upon your own individual health and that of the planet. This is not a criticism of people's eating habits. It is a window into the fast food and highly processed food industry which is having such a negative impact upon people and our planet.

Chapter 1

The Human Cell

INTRODUCTION

It is very important to have some understanding of just how our body functions. So let's begin with a human cell.

The human body is a chemical refinery made up of water (70%), minerals, vitamins, fibrous material and ash. Ash is the waste material from the refinery activity. When we die, some people think, our soul or spirit leaves the body, which has been its home whilst on earth, and the body then expires, leaving only the remnants of what was once a miraculous chemical machine made from trillions of cells, all miraculous and all little refineries themselves. If you don't believe in a soul, it really does not matter, except that it becomes a little more difficult when trying to understand how some people recover from a chronic illness and others with the same illness don't: but that is another story.

Before we set about understanding diet, we must learn a little more about the human cell. When our cells start to malfunction the whole body begins to malfunction. If our cells are healthy the whole body is healthy. We must look after the health of our cells.

The human cell is like a walled city. The wall is known as the membrane and has the remarkable ability to keep out or eject unwanted substances while allowing desirable materials in the form of enzymes and chemicals to enter. Inside there is a mass of structures or "factories", each with its own membrane and containing the same properties. In the middle stands the nucleus, the "cathedral" of hereditary information, which is transferred to all "offspring" or "daughter" cells. Cells die after they have reproduced daughter cells. New ones are being created all the time and old ones are dying all the time. Cell division multiplies the number of cells, which is required to replace dead cells in a process known as mitosis but every new cell has our inherited DNA[1] and it is this, which gives us our individuality and physical appearance.

The DNA molecule is the largest in the cell and carries information in a 4-letter alphabet.

Each cell contains about 30,000 million letters, equivalent to 1,000 books of 1,000 pages! This is our inherited computer. It is worth remembering that the fertilising cells (sperm and ova) only inherit half each of our DNA so that when they combine the whole amount of DNA is produced in the combination, half from the mother and half from the father. But no one can decide on which

50% the offspring inherits from each parent. It would be interesting if that were possible!

It is obvious that the cell membrane should be kept healthy otherwise it loses control over what is kept in and kept out.

Inside the cell are "factories" each producing different materials.

CELL FACTORIES

One of the most important mechanisms is the "sodium pump"[2] which pumps out sodium, an acid mineral, from the cell keeping the internal level of potassium, an alkaline mineral, higher than sodium. The cell cannot function efficiently if it is saturated with sodium because it becomes too acidic.[3]

The nucleus is another "factory" which produces all the information needed for the structure and function of every cell type in the body. It contains all the information for making, transporting and locating proteins and enzymes.

Other factories within the cell modify, manufacture, sort, transport, break down and store proteins, produce energy, protect, repair and express genetic information.

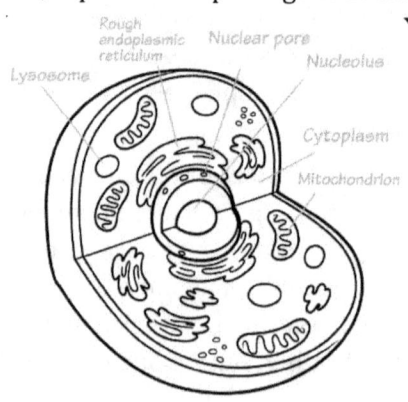

When seen under a powerful microscope the structures in the cell are absolutely astonishing and look more like a science fiction landscape.

CELL ACTIVITY

All cell activity is biochemical and it is very busy and diverse and embraces the breakdown of protein, carbohydrate and fat. Fat, for example, is broken down into cholesterol, fatty acids, phospholipids and steroids which all have to be synthesised into thousands of different enzyme proteins contained in the cells.

Protein is broken down into amino acids, which are used to make hormones such as adrenaline, and special chemical messengers like serotonin, which are active in the brain which keeps us cheerful while the information in the brain is being organised efficiently. If there is a lack of serotonin the person feels a bit "down" because the brain is not working so efficiently. The cell synthesises, manufactures, absorbs, excretes, transports and responds to many thousands of chemical products. It is hard but imagine thousands of chemical plants all operating together and controlled by one "cathedral" factory, the nucleus, which stamps its patent upon all products and you get some distance to understanding the phenomenal complexity of one single human cell.

Our body is made up of trillions of them so it is easy to see that if we do not look after them our body just "under functions" and leaves us feeling tired and lacklustre.

METABOLISM

This means a state in which the various biochemical processes are continuous, the concentrations of all the chemicals do not change much and the cellular structures are well maintained. If our metabolism is too rapid, we feel a sense of tension or stress and if it is too slow, we feel sluggish and tired. The thyroid gland has an important part to play in this process.

COMMUNICATION

Apart from maintaining themselves cells also specialise in specific functions as they are constantly in touch with each other via a sort of cell networking version of Twitter, Tik Tok or Facebook! When one cell demands something, another gives it. There is constant communication between cells, constant production, constant transport and maintenance. An example of this is the activity of the thyroid gland,[4] which needs iodine to function, so, when the thyroid gland ceases to produce enough thyroxin, triggers elsewhere in the body produce chemical messengers, which stimulate the thyroid gland to produce more thyroxin.

CONTROL

The only control over cell activity is through what we eat, drink, inhale or from drugs. Pharmaceutical companies spend billions on researching new ways of intervening in cell control mechanisms and cell communication so that their function is suppressed or altered.

The difference between conventional medicine and alternative medicine is that alternative medicine aims to assist in the repair of damaged cells by removing the cause of the damage. This involves the removal of poisons or toxins whilst conventional medicine often suppresses cell activity by intervening in its function and communication, e.g. anti - inflammatory or anti-depressant drugs.[5] This reflects health service thinking which treats the symptom, not the cause.

POWER

Much of what we eat contains hydrogen. You've heard of the H bomb? Well, each of our cells has a mini "bomb" utilising hydrogen to produce energy using a cell mechanism known as the "respiratory chain",[6] which takes hydrogen and oxygen to form water. This is where much energy is released.

Hydrogen is the ultimate fantastically efficient fuel because it releases so much energy per unit of weight of hydrogen consumed. It could be used to power aircraft if it was safe and as we know, it powers massively destructive bombs. It also produces the body's energy, heat and strength by producing an energy currency known as ATP (Adenosintriphosphate).

WHAT MAKES ENERGY?

The most vulnerable parts of the cell are its enzymes (chemicals), its membrane (outer skin) and its nucleus (the epicentre) Many medications and toxins are specific enzyme inhibitors and others are enzyme destroyers. Whole enzyme processes can fall victim to toxic attack. The most vulnerable of these is the combination citric acid cycle[7] and respiratory chain because they generate the cell's energy.

The process involves the cell's protein manufacturing mechanism and is a bit like a mini refinery, which takes raw materials and produces others.

Krebs[8] was the first person to discover in detail how our energy is manufactured. It is very complicated but requires Vitamin C, Magnesium (Mg) Manganese (Mn) and much more.

If our diet does not contain sufficient Vit C, Mg, Mn, Iron etc. the 'Sodium Pump' will not function efficiently, allowing the cell to slowly become acidic. The result can be a feeling of fatigue, and many of us tend to eat when we feel tired, in search of more energy, so it's important to know WHAT to eat to restore energy. If it's fast food, which is highly acidic, the energy shot can be effective; but not for long.

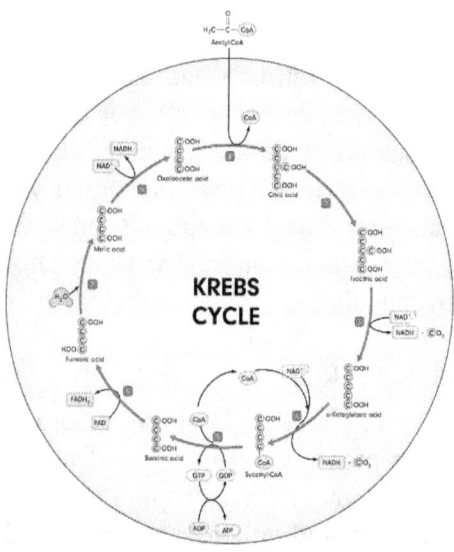

When the cell loses its capacity to produce sufficient energy every other system begins its degenerative process towards death. This is known as the chronic state. We know how it feels because we have all felt exhausted from time to time but when the fatigue seems to go on forever, it has become chronic. Some toxins can have a very rapid and devastating effect, e.g. cyanide[9] which blocks one single enzyme, cytochrome oxidase, without which the body's cells are unable to use oxygen causing cell suffocation and a pretty rapid and unpleasant death.

On a less pessimistic note, when we feel tired, we are experiencing a dip in cell energy production. Our cells have become toxic and the citric cycle and respiratory chain are under attack and malfunctioning.

When the nucleus is attacked by toxins, our DNA, and the inconceivable numbers of complex messages stored there are altered. The messaging system gets scrambled causing all sorts of problems. These toxins are called mutagens because DNA alterations affect the daughter cells creating mutations or mutant cells. Cancerous cells are "mutant", and produce abnormal material.

However, DNA repair and restoration is available through the cell's amazing array of "doctor" enzymes[10] which snip out and replace damaged DNA. Unfortunately, chronic or long-term abuse will eventually overcome these remarkable healing enzymes. In short, the body heals itself given half a chance. It possesses its own health service, and it's free, so why would you abuse it?

If we stop poisoning our damaged cells, repair can take place but the longer toxification lasts, the harder it is to repair. One particular toxin, sugar,[11] does more harm in the body than we imagine. Excess sugar in the diet should be avoided so beware fizzy drinks, sweets, chocolates, cakes, biscuits, processed wheat: bread, pizza, pasta, alcohol and refined starches such as crisps.

Avoid salt too! When a cell becomes poisoned with toxins, which reduces cell energy, the sodium pump[12] fails, so sodium begins to flood the cell, making it very hard for the cell to function normally. Sodium attracts water, so the cell becomes diluted and increasingly acidic, reducing the value of other minerals and eventually leading to cell damage and cell death.

CELL FOOD

Cells need minerals such as magnesium for the Krebbs cycle, which manufactures energy. Many other trace minerals are needed but in the correct quantities. It is surprising to learn that we need and indeed consume minerals such as iron, zinc, manganese, potassium, phosphorous, calcium, boron, silicon and more. We also require a wide range of vitamins and if these elements are not in correct amounts the cell malfunctions. We also need phytonutrients, which come from plants in minute quantities.

ACTION

If you can appreciate just how vulnerable each one of your cells is you will understand the vulnerability of the total sum of those cells. The sum of those cells is you.

So what must be done to maintain cell health and therefore your total health?

1. Avoid toxic exposure.

Don't add any extra chemicals to your food such as salt.

2. Avoid a deficiency of nutrients and a deficiency of essential fatty acids.

Eat a well-balanced diet.

3. Avoid nutritional imbalances.

Too much sodium and not enough potassium. Eat a well-balanced diet.

4. Consume plenty of antioxidants.

Vitamins C, E, and selenium. Eat an even better balanced diet.

5. Do not consume excess sugar, wheat, dairy, caffeine and alcohol.

6. Learn and enjoy to cook properly and then you will love your food which is, after all, the essence of life.

If you are not well, if you are stressed or if you are not happy with your health, it is almost always due to toxicity in your cells. Remember, toxins also arise from emotional situations such as jealousy, grief, anger, stress and despair.

Nutrients from a good dietary source are there to protect you and to maintain good health. If your toxic levels are too high for these to be effective, powerful naturopathic cleansing procedures may have to be employed. This involves elimination of those toxins, which are making you unwell, and the reinstatement of healthy and efficient cells. Rarely does orthodox medicine follow this approach.

Chapter 2

Acidity in the Diet

WHAT IS ACIDITY?

Complicated it may be but it makes an enormous difference if we have an understanding of acidity in the diet. It enables us to make informed judgements about the food we eat and the drinks we consume.

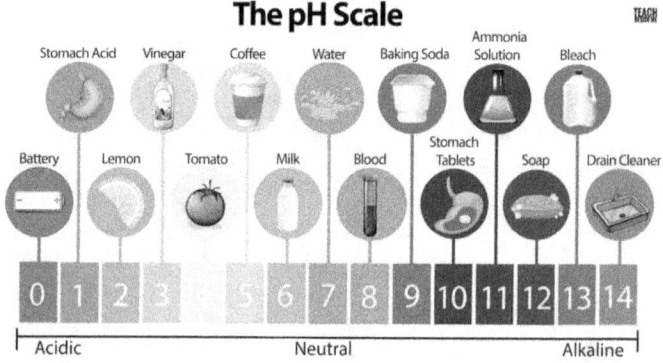

We have to understand a pH scale, which measures acidity.[13]

Water, which has a neutral balance, has an equal amount of acid and alkali. In Chinese circles this is known as Yin, which is alkaline (potassium) and Yang, which is acid (sodium).

Potassium promotes but sodium inhibits oxidation. Oxidation is required for the manufacture of energy. In chronic diseases there are usually high levels of sodium leading to low levels of energy. Alkaline foods contain potassium.

Natural balance is measured as having a pH of -7. A pH which lies between -7 and 0, is increasingly acid and a pH which lies between -7 and -14 is increasingly alkaline. The stomach secretes hydrochloric acid to digest food and this is a very strong acid. When it becomes too acid and produces "heartburn" we might take Milk of Magnesia, which is "chalky" and is alkaline.

Acid = pH 0

Neutral = pH -7

Alkaline = pH -14

The somewhat alarming fact is that the body's blood likes to be just very slightly alkaline with a pH of -7.4. Even minor changes are undesirable leading to a coma or convulsions.

There is not much room for error and the body's mechanisms for ensuring the right balance of pH must be cared for and maintained.

The body is full of acids and alkaline all being balanced at a pH of -7.4 in a system called titration. This uses buffer systems. For example when blood transfers from the arteries to the veins it produces carbon dioxide which enters the cells and combines with the water inside them to make carbonic acid, which is a weak acid.

When we breathe out we exhale carbon dioxide and when we exercise we exhale more carbon dioxide, reducing the acid in the cells, so our pH rises and we reduce the chances of acidosis or too much acid. So taking some exercise is important.

There are very many buffer systems all trying to maintain the pH balance but in spite of these buffers if we eat the wrong foods, our pH balance moves towards -7 and we become acidic, prone to anxiety, and if this continues, we become unhealthy and lose energy.

ACIDOSIS

When we eat suppressive foods such as meat, dairy, wheat and processed foods, we upset the mineral balances in our bodies. Minerals have acidic or alkaline qualities and so they are able to raise or lower our pH level.

Acidity in the cells forces some important minerals out of the cells ensuring that the cell does not function properly. The mineral composition of the cells changes and this includes cells of the bones. If the mineral status of cells is depleted, our energy levels fade and the sodium pump[12] fails too, allowing too much sodium to remain in the cell, expelling potassium, the major alkaline. The sodium attracts water, so the cell becomes acidic and destroys the minerals, which the cell so desperately needs.

Acidification of the bone cells leads to the expulsion of sodium, potassium, calcium and magnesium. This leads to decalcification of the skeleton and eventually bone diseases such as osteoporosis.

When we choose a diet which includes acid forming foods such as milk, wheat, processed foods and meat, and where we choose to eat foods which upset our mineral balance such as caffeine, sugar, alcohol and wheat, and if we add salt to our food, we are inevitably going to increase the acidity in our cells and our blood. This leads to more mineral losses in bone cells and eventually ill health and chronic diseases such as arthritis, osteoporosis, heart failure, strokes and a feeling of stiffness, soreness and fatigue. I often ask myself why so many people eat themselves into chronic illness and can only conclude that it is just sheer ignorance of food content and a misunderstanding of what good food is.

WHAT SHOULD WE DO?

The body likes to be slightly alkaline with an acidic digestive system and acidic skin. We should eat more food from plants, apart from wheat, and less food from animals, apart from fish.

Animal protein creates an alkaline environment in the intestines, which are meant to be acidic to aid digestion.[13] If the gut becomes too alkaline, the bacteria create a putrefying environment resulting in the production of toxins in the gut, which damage the bowel and the liver. Additionally, animal foods usually contain sulphur,[14] which forms sulphuric acid and adds to acidosis. Animal foods also contain phosphorous[15] which produces phosphoric acid. These acids raise acidity in the body. Animal foods also contain arachidonic acid so acidity is increased once more. Animal foods contain very little fibre. Fibre is important to ensure that the time it takes for our food to pass through us is not delayed.

As can be seen from this information animal food can lead to poor health if consumed on a regular basis and in large quantities. Vegetarians tend to suffer less than heavy meat eaters from most of the chronic illnesses.[16]

Plant foods are low in proteins causing less noxious fumes caused by putrefaction and are rich in fibre ensuring a good transit time and undelayed elimination. They contain valuable minerals and vitamins, almost no fat and they do not upset the balance of acid in the digestive tract. They are low in sulphur so instead of creating sulphuric acid they contain potassium which is alkaline and which is what the body requires.

Wheat and cereals produce phytic acid in the bowel, which reduces the absorption of minerals.

The advice is simple. Eat lots of vegetables and fruit and do not eat lots of meat and dairy foods.

FIBRE CONTENT IN FOODS[17]

PLANT FOOD	ANIMAL FOOD	JUNK FOOD
Average of 49 vegetables 27.1 gms per 100	0 gms per 100	Average of 63 Junk Foods 3.65 gms per 100

Dr. Denis Burkitt who discovered Burkitt's Lymphoma was also responsible for proving beyond doubt that 'Western Diseases' are, more than anything else, the result of a lack of fibre in 'Western Diets'. In a lecture given in 1984, he names some of those non-infective diseases – Appendicitis, Diverticular disease, Cancer of the bowel, Hiatus Hernia, Coronary Heart disease, Varicose Veins, Diabetes, Gall stones and finally Obesity. None of these were common in sub Saharan Africa at a time where diets contained high levels of fibre. Burkitt battled for years to convince authorities to accept his findings but, being a humble man, he also recognised a glaring fault in the conventional medical world.

'... if we are to eradicate Western diseases ... it will not be by improving treatment but by eradicating causes. And one of the causes I am emphasising is a faulty diet. (Fast Foods?)

Let me put it another way. Here we have water running from a tap. There is a flood on the floor. Two highly dedicated, well-trained gentlemen have a single motive in life – to try to keep the floor dry. They mop fourteen hours a day. It never occurs to them to turn off the tap.

The tap water represents the cause of the diseases that are potentially preventable and are filling our hospital beds. Half a century ago I spent five years as a medical student learning how to mop floors. When I qualified as a doctor I studied for post-graduate diplomas on the use of electronic mops and improved brushes. I mopped furiously and happily for thirty years before I began to look at the taps.

In England today (1984) something like 99% of health expenditure goes on floor mopping. 1% on prevention, on turning off taps. In USA it is a third of 1%. As Ogden Nash said, "We are making great progress but we are heading in the wrong direction."

Quote from 'Fibre Man, The Life Story of Dr. Denis Burkitt', *A book by Brian Kellock, A Lion Paperback, 1985*

We see today the continued folly of mopping floors at ever-increasing expense but the water continues to flow onto the floor. And now, not just in the more prosperous West but around the planet in countries that cannot afford mechanical mops.

Whatever happened to common sense?

Chapter 3

The Toxic Load

UNNATURAL CHEMICAL TOXINS

The food we eat contains many and various chemicals, which are used to rid us of toxins.[18] These include well-known benefits such as antioxidants. Our immune system is a kind of police force, which patrols the body looking for toxic or alien invaders such as chemical pollutants found in petrol fumes and paints. When these are discovered, they are captured, bundled up and expelled.

In addition, when the body burns fuel, using oxygen, there is a residue or "ash" which if left in the cells becomes toxic. All these potentially dangerous substances need to be neutralised or eliminated from the body through either the blood stream or the lymphatic system.

It is our responsibility to avoid ingesting or absorbing toxins where at all possible and of course this includes the toxins within our food chain.

So, where do all these horrible toxins exist? We must, by the way, accept viruses and bacteria as toxins in the same way as we do the dangers of snakebites and wasp stings.

Solvents

Paints, varnishes, antifreeze, adhesives, cleaning agents and acetone are contained in this group. The most commonly used chemicals in this group are methanol, carbon tetrachloride and benzene. They affect the central nervous system. Some solvents are used in the food processing business, for example the extraction of vegetable oils from oil seeds and in decaffeinating coffee and tea.

If large doses of any of these toxins are ingested very nasty results occur, but this is rare. Instead, we ingest minute amounts, frequently over long periods of time but no one knows what the long-term results are. Not yet anyway, but it is as well to avoid them where possible and as a good example, don't drink decaffeinated tea and coffee regularly.

Refrigerants

As greenhouse gases these are being phased out not because they are dangerous to our health but for the health of the planet. However, fluorine and chlorine were used and both are cardiac stimulants, so I wonder why fluoride is being used in some water supplies?

Cleaning Materials

Soap is not good to eat so we don't but detergents contain sulphurs, which require thorough rinsing after washing up.

Pesticides

Some people remember the disastrous consequence of DDT yet the agrochemical industry still insists that pesticides are not dangerous to humans. Horrible chemical killers such as aldrin, endrin and benzene hexachloride are used on fields of food to destroy insects. An insect is minute compared to a human in size so very little chemical is required to kill it but for humans the long-term effects of ingesting these chemicals include anorexia, anaemia, tremors, weakness, headaches, nervous tension, irritability and insomnia, skin rashes, memory loss and low sperm production in males.

Other pesticides interfere with nerve impulse transmission and affect the salivary, sweat and tear glands and also the eyes, digestive organs, respiratory system, bladder, nervous system and cardiovascular system.

Insecticides also include toxins from pyrethrum and chrysanthemum through chemical synthesis, which affect the nervous system leading to dizziness, burning, and itching of the skin as experienced by very many Chinese people working in agriculture some years ago. If these chemicals are ingested, they cause nausea, vomiting, palpitations, fatigue and blurring of vision.

Herbicides and Fungicides

The number of different chemicals used to kill weeds and fungus is enormous and all of them are dangerous and poisonous. Consumption is low but they are part of the farming industry and are also used for road and path maintenance. The chemicals are washed down the drains and into the water system and into our rivers and therefore into our drinking water, and try as we may, we cannot get rid of all of it from our food and drinking water chain.

As far back as the 1980s a report suggested that they could be responsible for 60% of dietary carcinogenic risk and that 90% of all agricultural fungicides have been shown to be carcinogenic in animal models.

The worrying thing here is that there is not enough pressure to bear on the use of weed killers and fungicides on our farmlands. The chemicals are hugely poisonous and yet seep into our food chain.

Rodenticides

Not many people consume rat or mouse poison and since we don't usually eat rats or mice either, the poisons used for controlling rodents don't usually find their way into the food chain. However, warfarin is used in rat poison. It has also been used as an anticoagulant or blood thinner in humans. There have been many reports such as that found in The Library of Medicine which explains that Vitamin E which is a Vitamin K inhibitor (Vitamin K controls blood clotting) can act in the same way without side effects so why do some doctors turn away from Vitamin E? Vitamin E is abundant in nuts, vegetables, fruit and oils.

Fertilisers

Nitrogen, phosphates and potash are the common fertilisers and are just nutrients for plants. Nitrogen increases the nitrate and nitrate content of the water running off from agricultural soils and into waterways and water supplies. These may create nitrosamines, which are highly toxic. Unless water treatment can remove nitrosamines, which have been associated with cancer, they become dangerous if there is a build up in the body.

SUMMARY

It is not unreasonable to be worried at the amount of chemicals that could enter the food chain. Even though the amounts are small, unless our immune system is able to eliminate them from the body, they will build up in the cells and create problems. Is it fair to accept that the modern food industry is able to eradicate all traces of the poisonous chemicals used in food production especially in processed food production?

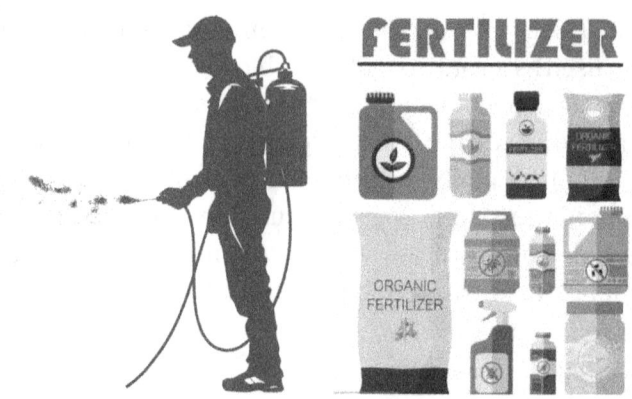

Processed foods eaten over long periods of time can have hazardous effects on our health.

Chapter 4

Macro Nutrients

INTRODUCTION

Macronutrients are the bulk ingredients that the body requires to function healthily and it is within these that the micronutrients such as vitamins and minerals are found.[19]

PROTEIN

Most relatively inactive people need no more than 80 gms of protein per day. Protein is required for building up and maintaining the cells and aiding in their replacement as well as providing us with hormones, enzymes and amino acids. We only need small amounts of protein and the excess protein is converted to ammonia and then to uric acid before being eliminated through the kidneys.[19]

Unwanted protein puts a huge strain on the kidneys which eliminates it and because the digestion of protein uses up more energy than any other food, it is a waste of your energy and money to eat too much of it. Excess protein can also lead to ill health including liver, bowel and kidney diseases.

Fish is one of my preferred protein sources because it is light and contains high levels of minerals, essential oils and is usually low in dangerous fats. Fish are vulnerable to pollution and need to be cooked thoroughly.

Other rich sources of protein are meats, eggs, cheese and milk. It is important to appreciate that much junk food is protein rich. It is no coincidence that many burgers come with cheese since a cow produces both meat and milk. Ideal for profits!

CARBOHYDRATES

About 50% of our diet should be carbohydrates because it gives us our energy through sugar. However, sugar comes as a slow or fast release source of energy. If the carbohydrate is processed, as in white bread, it releases its sugar quickly, whereas brown rice, which is not as processed, releases its sugar slowly.[20]

The reason for this is because the processing eliminates the fibre, which is often indigestible, and destroys the germ, which contains all the nutrients and also takes a long time to digest. Processed carbohydrates give us almost instant energy and not much else, whereas unprocessed carbohydrates give us almost the same amount of energy over a longer period of time but with the added benefits of nutrients and fibre.

The GI or Glycaemic Index is the measure of this process and tells us that everything is measured against the 100% conversion rate of neat processed sugar into glucose. A baked potato has an index of 85% making it the second highest G Indexed food that we know of. Lentils on the other hand convert at a rate of only 29%.

So what?

Well, when sugar enters the blood stream it has to be absorbed into our cells. If we have too much sugar in our blood, we could have a fit. High blood sugar levels lead to hyperactivity but excess sugar leads to fits. It is insulin that attaches the sugar to the cells and it is very efficient so no sooner has this happened than the body is calling for more sugar.

Too little sugar in the blood can lead to a coma in excessive cases but in any case leads to fatigue, so the body will crave sugar when it is feeling tired. The fluctuation between high and low sugar levels can eventually exhaust the insulin glands and insulin production which can mean the gradual onset of diabetes.[21]

We must protect the glands that produce the insulin, which are located in the pancreas.

Having a trickle of sugar from carbohydrates is the way to manage this and it cannot be done with processed carbohydrate foods such as white bread or white rice and pasta.

The alternatives are brown unprocessed rice, millet, oats or genuine whole meal bread using unprocessed flour.

Carbohydrates can come from some root vegetables, beans, pulses and lentils and is present in fruit sugar (fructose). And also in lactose which is the sugar in milk.

FATS AND OILS

There is a major problem concerning fats because there are different types and furthermore, they can change very quickly and easily into dangerous substances depending on packaging, heating and storage, so it is necessary to understand just a few basic things before trying to estimate how much should be consumed.[22]

There are three main types of fats: saturated, monounsaturated and polyunsaturated.

Saturated Fats

These are not essential to the body but almost impossible to avoid. Over-consumption can lead to heart and arterial problems but anyone who consumes sufficient supplies of micronutrients from plant foods is usually capable of metabolising saturated fats, thereby reducing their danger. Nevertheless, it is just foolish to consume large quantities of saturated fat but even more foolish to eat these fats without also consuming a high quantity of vegetables.

Typical foods with high levels of saturated fat are butter, lamb, pork and beef.

Unsaturated Fats

Some of these are essential to consume but only if consumed in the correct proportions. There are two categories here, mono and polyunsaturated fats.

Monounsaturated Fats

These include oils from olives, seeds, rapeseed and castor oil.

Polyunsaturated Fats

Most plants contain some polyunsaturated fat or oil, typically sunflowers. Some of these are essential for consumption but the problems arise in the production, cooking, storage and handling of them.

Unless these fats are unaltered, which makes production very difficult, they can become toxic.

When margarine is made, the original vegetable oil has to be hardened because it would be difficult to spread as oil. Many Europeans however use olive oil as a spread. They simply drizzle the oil over their bread and salads. This may serve them well as they use almost no margarine.

The alteration of oil to margarine is called hydrogenation and this creates something more like butter and therefore more like a saturated fat.

When cooking oil is heated its chemical construction is altered into something increasingly toxic so that chips and fish heated in an astonishingly hot oil come with inherent dangers. Reports have been written about the dangers of this process with special attention given to the manufacture of crisps.

Even leaving cooking oil on a windowsill is not advisable due to the sun's rays heating it through a transparent plastic bottle and changing its chemistry. I do not wish to dwell on this matter too long but oil stored in transparent plastic is not advisable because the chemistry of the plastic container also changes. If you leave a plastic container in the sun for a few days you will notice that it becomes more brittle and eventually flakes and crumbles away. That is because the plastic has lost some of its chemicals and may have been leached out into the oil used for cooking.

Just be careful with the way you use polyunsaturated fats because we do need them but they should not be altered.

Why is olive oil stored in brown bottles? I think the answer is now clear.

Fat is useful because it is easy to store in the body and when required it is easily converted into energy.

Saturated fat has almost no nutritional value at all but is good for energy supply. Some unsaturated fats such as omega-3 and omega-6 are essential because they can be used for things other than energy.

Today we face a problem of imbalance because if we have too much omega-6, readily available in meats, sunflower oil, corn oil, margarines, cooking oils, dressings, and so on, without balanced amounts of omega-3 oil which comes from fish, linseeds or flaxseeds, the dangers are greater than having a deficiency of both.

Balance is the key. It is of the greatest important to consume some omega-3 even if this means taking supplements.

Fats and oils are difficult to measure but as a generalisation, animal fats which include milk and butter are dangerous in large quantities and vegetable oils and fats such as cooking oils and margarine can become equally harmful if heated, exposed to light or just hardened or consumed in far greater quantities than fish oil or linseed oil. About 12 to 15 percent of our daily diet should be made up of fats and oils. Saturated fat should be kept to a minimum. We should also keep omega-6 and omega-3 on a ratio of 3:1, within the 12 to 15 per cent of fats and oils.

Olive oil is known as monounsaturated fat and is better than margarine to cook with at low temperatures.

FIBRE

Fibre does not exist in food that we consume from animals and fish. It is only available in fruit, vegetables and unprocessed whole meal bread, oats, unprocessed rice and millet and in pulses, lentils, beans and almost all unprocessed plant food.

Without fibre our digestive system can become clogged up leading to constipation and eventually to more serious diseases of the digestive tract from the mouth to the exit.[23]

Fibre should make up about 20–25% of our diet – a lot of vegetables. It is generally not digestible but it ensures that the food we eat creates some friction on the gut wall so that the digestive muscles have something to get hold of when they squeeze the semi-digested food (chime) along the large intestine.

It helps to maintain a clean intestine, which aids the manufacture of good bacteria, and it also ensures that the transit time of food through the intestines is never too sluggish. All of this enables the good bacteria to flourish.

I am absolutely adamant that the vast majority of chronic diseases start in the digestive tract and that if we do consume sufficient fibre the chances of developing these diseases are greatly reduced.

Chapter 5

Food Values

WEIGHTS AND MEASURES

1 Kilogram is 2.2 pounds and there are 1,000 gms in a kilogram.

1 Gram is only 1/28.4 of an ounce and there are 1,000 milligrams in a gram.

1 milligrams is 0.001 of a gram and is the smallest amount that can be weighed on scales. It is a tiny weight but 1 microgram is 1,000 times smaller!

There are a million micrograms in a gram and some of the mineral amounts that we need are measured in micrograms. This, however, does not make them any less important. It just reflects the staggering way our bodies are made when such minuscule amounts of minerals can make the difference between good and poor health.

Another interesting point is that the body only requires about 500 gms of food as dried weight, daily.

Dried weight means that all the water, which is valueless, has been taken out.

100 gms is about 3.5 ounces in imperial weight so we only need about 17.5 ounces of dried food a day after all the water has been extracted. This proves just how much water there is in our food and that just over one pound of food (dried) is enough to give us a day's worth of energy and all the nutrients we need to live normally. Amazing!

All these values are water free. It's the only way to compare food and nutritional values of food and to give an example, a pound of fresh lettuce will present only a fraction of the nutritional value compared to a pound of carrots! As a further example, a helping of baked beans weighs about 140 gms but when the water content has been removed it only weighs about 40 gms. So just over two thirds have no nutritional value.

Using this example, 40 gms (dried) of baked beans contains in gms the following ingredients:

Protein	7.3 g
Fats	0.8 g
Carbohydrates	21.5 g
Starch	13.2 g
Sugars	8.3 g
Fibre	9.7g
Calories	117.9

When the starch and sugar numbers are added they equate to the carbohydrate figure.

Let's take this example a stage further because looking at these figures we appear to have a pretty good food.

We are trying to achieve the following balance of nutrients in our diet:

Protein – 15%

Fat – 15%

Carbohydrate – 50%

Fibre – 20%

Baked beans give us:

Protein – 18%

Fat – 2%

Carbohydrates – 54%

Fibre – 25%

So, low fat, high fibre, relatively low protein and not excessive carbohydrates.

Carbohydrates come as starch and sugars and convert to give us energy, although, if the energy is not needed the unused sugars become a menace and are stored as fat. It is all about balance and requirement. A lumberjack requires much more energy than a computer consultant and therefore these needs must be part of the dietary organisation.

The above example shows that baked beans are a good source of food. *But is that the whole picture?*

If we look at the vitamin and mineral values we begin to see a different picture.

Minerals in milligms.

Remember that 1,000 mg = 1g

Phosphorous	140 mg
Salt	744 mg
Potassium	435 mg
Calcium	74 mg
Magnesium	43 mg
Iron	2 mg
Zinc	0.7 mg
Copper	0 mg
Manganese	0.4 mg

VITAMINS

Vit A (Retinol)	0 mg
Vit A (Carotene)	104 mg
D	0 mg
B6	0.2 mg
B12	0 mg
C	0 mg
B1 (Thiamine)	0.1 mg
B2 (Riboflavin)	0.1 mg
B3 (Niacin)	0.1 mg
Folate	31 mg *
Biotin	3.5 mg
B5	0.3 mg

* Folate (Vitamin B9) has almost the same impact as Vitamin B12. The meat industry reminds its audience that without consumption, there would be a deficiency in B12 consumption. Baked beans contain the Vitamin Folate (B9) as do other sources – dark green vegetables, fruits, beans, nuts and seeds.

Even without knowing anything about the amount of minerals and vitamins we ought to be consuming on a daily basis it is clear that baked beans have little to offer in vitamins and apart from high levels of salt and a poor ratio of salt to potassium leading to acidosis, it has little to offer in the way of minerals either.

Is it a good food? In my estimation it is not good nor is it the worst sort of food to eat but it typifies processed foods. The occasional intake will do no lasting harm but many households see it as a staple food and that is worrying because it will destroy the acid to alkaline balance, which erodes the immune system.

MEASUREMENTS AND INGREDIENTS IN ALL THE FOLLOWING PAGES

We are assuming that the average person should consume about 500 gms of food when all the water has been extracted. This is known as dry matter.

I recommend 250 gms should be carbohydrates supplying us with energy. 100 gms should be fibre.

Protein and fat or oils make up 75 gms each.

The content of food will give us about 1,800–2,500 calories of energy a day.

The figures I use for the macronutrients are for a portion or an average helping so that a portion of broccoli will give us 2.5 gms of protein and 1 gramme of carbohydrates. We need 250 gms of carbohydrates a day so broccoli is a good food for slimmers!

The micronutrients of vitamins and minerals are measured in mcg and mg.

HOW DO I MEASURE VITAMINS AND MINERALS?

It all gets too complicated to remember exactly what each of the macro and micronutrients are but it is sufficient to understand that a balance of all of them is required. If you do not consume sufficient nutrients for any length of time your body may be able to compensate for a while but will eventually begin to suffer from their depletion.

The secret is to have a balanced diet covering all aspects of food sources, which will almost guarantee that you are consuming the right amounts of vitamins and minerals as well as the macronutrients. This is no more than common sense.

Instead of giving the precise values of all the foods listed in the following chapters, I am going to use a simple system that will show what minerals and vitamins the foods possess.

Although the vitamins and minerals for these foods may not be coded they can possess additional good values in micrograms and phytonutrients.

It does not matter that the food is measured in dry matter because practitioners, who design diets for their clients, use this. More importantly, you should be able to understand what is available to you in each of the most common foods in nutritional value and for this purpose the following values are for an average portion or a helping.

But everyone's portions are different so the figures are only a rough guide. Its purpose is to give an idea of just how important it is to have a balanced diet in order that the right amount of nutrients and minerals are consumed with the right amount of fibre, proteins, oils and carbohydrates. This is not rocket science and it is easy to gauge whether a diet is adequate or poor, brilliant or average. Try it and see how you get on. I think you will be quite surprised at just how much we take for granted and at how many of us eat a far from nutritious diet.

I use 3 stars *** for good food, 2 stars ** for average foods and just 1 star * for poor foods.

Chapter 6

Vitamins and Minerals

Recommended daily intakes of minerals and vitamins for adults

There are differing opinions regarding the intake of vitamins and minerals. Factors include age, workplace activity, climate and, of course, vested interests! My figures are based upon a reasonably healthy person hoping to remain healthy.

Magnesium (Mg)	450 milligms (mg)
Zinc (Zn)	17 mg
Iron (Fe)	10 mg
Copper (Cu)	2 mg
Manganese (Mn)	4 mg
Chromium (Cr)	50 microgms (mcg)
Selenium (Se)	50 mcg
Salt (Na)	1,000 mg
Potassium (K)	5,000 mg
Calcium (Ca)	1,000 mg

THE IMPORTANCE OF MINERALS

MAGNESIUM

Magnesium is essential for life because chlorophyll needs magnesium for photosynthesis. This is why magnesium is so abundant in green leafy vegetables, for example.

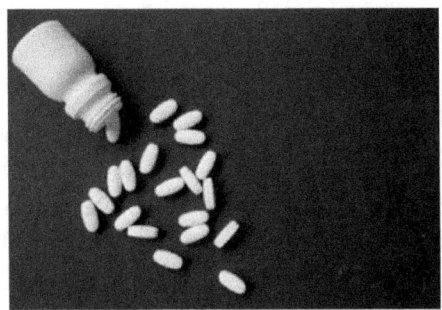

After potassium, it is the most important metal in the cell and is essential for nerve impulse and muscular function. It is also a co-factor in a very large number of enzymes. Its most important role is in the production of ATP, which is the body's energy source and is manufactured in our cells.

Much of it resides in our bones but makes up less than 0.3% of bone, whereas calcium makes up 21% and phosphorous about 10% of all bone. Nevertheless, it is hugely important to us.

There are lots of conflicting views as to how much we need. Even different countries cannot agree. Most practitioners with a nutrition background believe that about 450 mg daily is required. Most people are deficient in magnesium, even by the lowest levels of requirement, and yet no action is taken to correct this.

Most Western populations are affected by fatigue and one reason for this is a deficiency in magnesium. Magnesium content in fruits and vegetables has diminished over the previous 50 years due to food processing and the use of pesticides, fertilisation, modern agricultural technologies, and global warming. Magnesium is not alone in this decline. Most vitamins and minerals are affected in this way, to the overall detriment to the health of humanity.[24]

The best sources of magnesium are seeds, nuts, celery, vegetables, pulses and fish.

Shellfish have an abundance of magnesium but they also have a lot of salt.

A deficiency of magnesium can, if it occurs over a long period of time, lead to anxiety, hyperactivity, apprehension, tension, poor digestion, acidity, loss of energy, poor powers of detoxification, cell damage and deficient cell function leading to vulnerability from bacterial and viral attack and toxic damage and eventually to chronic disease. Stress, mental health, anxiety – ring any bells!?

SODIUM AND POTASSIUM

It is difficult to talk about sodium (salt) without including potassium because they work in conjunction with each other. Our body is more than 70% water and it will not function properly if the water balance is disturbed.

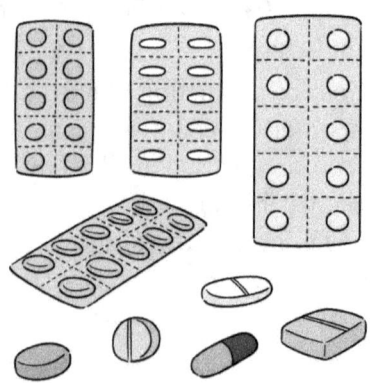

This is regulated by potassium and sodium working together and in the correct quantities. Too much of one and the water balance is upset with unpleasant consequences such as high blood pressure. This balance, 'homeostasis', is critical for the correct function of almost all the bodily functions and involves, in particular, the kidneys.

Sodium and potassium are known as macro minerals because we need a lot of them and their functions beyond water balance are to maintain the correct environment for other chemical changes to occur and to control water in and out of our cells and tissues. They are important for the maintenance of the structural and functional properties of proteins and they control nerve impulses and muscle contractions.

There are many other critical functions of these two metals but they are too numerous to list here. An imbalance of these minerals can lead to a host of outcomes such as nausea, vomiting, cramps, dizziness, exhaustion, listlessness, circulatory failure, mental confusion, irritability, oedema, muscle weakness, paralysis of the small intestine, heartbeat malfunction, headaches, joint pains and bone pain, and high blood pressure. The list continues but is too long to add here.

The most obvious sign of excess sodium is fatigue, which is a stark warning for our cells' ability to give us energy.

We need to eat about 5 times as much potassium as sodium, which is not difficult because potassium is found in vegetables in a good ratio to salt in favour of potassium. The problem we all face is in processed foods, which contain little or no potassium and too much salt.[25] This throws the sodium/potassium balance out of kilter and very rapidly damages our health.

The most helpful foods for getting the correct balance are fruits, leaf vegetables, tomatoes, potatoes, cauliflower, nuts, seeds, and root vegetables.

Foods which have much higher levels of salt are crustaceans and shellfish and of course processed foods because they disrupt the sodium/potassium balance.[26]

Baking powder, used in all manner of foods, has a ratio of 12,593 to 52 in favour of salt. Salted butter has a ratio of: 1005 to 17

A packet of chicken soup: 6429 to 284 Oxo cubes: 11,331 to 803

Bacon: 2,734 to 488

Marmite: 6032 to 3485

Smoked fish: 4296 to 1021

Sausages: 1698 to 314

Cornflakes: 1196 to 102

Doctors around the world have been in agreement for some time that excess salt added to our diet is not a good thing. It is unfortunate they do not go on to say with the same gusto, that potassium is absolutely essential for good health and that the salt/potassium ratio is what is important.

Too much salt and not enough potassium leads inexorably to acidity and low energy levels. And low energy levels leads to poor health as your immune system stutters.

CALCIUM

This important mineral is used to maintain bone strength and almost 99% of it is found in our bones but the 1% remaining is exceedingly valuable. 0.2% is stored in the blood and the soft tissues. The bone calcium acts as a reservoir so that the more important blood and tissue calcium can be restocked to maintain the right levels.

Apart from the manufacture of bone, calcium is used for muscle contraction, cell division, neurotransmitter release, egg fertilisation, activation of enzymes and endocrine secretion.

About 1,000 mg daily is required for most adults but young children need more and pregnant women need about 1200 mg.

The problems of deficiency do not arise if we eat a reasonable amount of vegetables and fruit and if we do not eat too much salt.

There is a problem from eating too much calcium because the effects of excess calcium are unpleasant and include arthritis, spondylitis, gallstones, renal stones and arterial atheroma.

Calcium is strongly linked to oestrogen because it requires this hormone in the making of bone so the healthy presence of calcium in our body depends upon other factors but eating plenty of vegetables and fruit and avoiding salty foods will certainly help to keep calcium levels correct.

ZINC

Very serious consequences arise from a deficiency of zinc. Essential as a co-factor in about 200 enzymes it assists in things like the digestion of proteins, repair to damaged DNA, preventing cell damage, strengthening bones, production of energy and so on.

It is also essential for normal growth rate, the normal function of the immune system, reproduction, the health of the central nervous system and mental health, blood sugar control, the circulatory system, for taste and smell and eyesight, and many others. It is responsible for the birth of normally formed babies and it is often the case that abnormal babies and abnormal births result from a zinc deficiency.

We need at least 15 mg daily and up to 30 mg for pregnant women and 40 mg for lactating women. The important thing is to consume no less than 15 mg daily and more if at all possible.

It is found in the highest quantities in eggs, liver, oysters, seeds, nuts, fish, pulses, vegetables, especially in endives, watercress and asparagus, oats, whole wheat and meats.

The things that deplete zinc are the contraceptive pill, sweeteners, steroids, fertilisation of farmland where nitrogen, phosphorous and potassium are used, alcohol, smoking and a sudden conversion to becoming a vegetarian.

IRON

As we all know, iron is essential for the transportation of oxygen. A deficiency of haem iron can lead to anaemia.

It is also related to poor digestive function leading to gastritis. Other problems include headaches, pins and needles in the toes and fingers, insomnia, giddiness, a fast pulse, dim vision, pimples and boils, weak muscles and heart murmurs.

We need 15 mg daily and perhaps a little less for women.

The main sources of iron in our diet are liver, meat, seeds, nuts, fish, pulses, vegetables, oats and fruit.

COPPER

Copper was once readily available in our food but since the introduction of modern farming methods this is no longer the case.

It is an essential ingredient as an enzyme co-factor. It is also important for neurotransmission and for the production of energy, for the manufacturing of structural connective tissues and it is an important antioxidant.

Deficiency can lead to bone deterioration, weak muscles, MS, irregular heartbeat, high cholesterol levels, heart attack, bulging arterial walls, poor hair quality, dementia, behavioural problems and mental instability.

There are dangers also related to excess copper in the body and this must be avoided just as rigorously as a deficiency. Copper is found in reasonable quantities in brown rice, pulses (especially Soya beans), vegetables (especially mushrooms), fruits, liver, fish, oysters, and nuts.

MANGANESE

No one quite knows what occurs if there is a major manganese deficiency because it has not been researched but we need between 2 and 3 mg daily. Some researchers believe we need as much as 20 mg. In any case it is required as an enzyme co-factor and for the production of thyroxin.

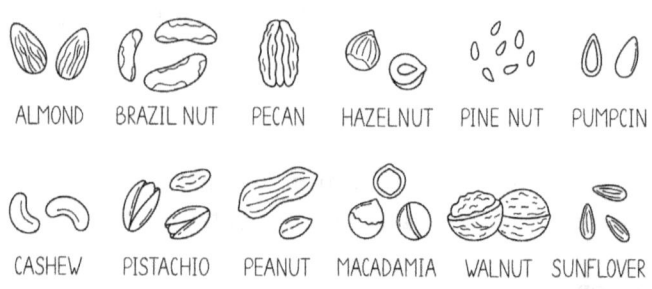

Deficiency can lead to stunted growth in children as it has a profound effect on the growth of bone mineralisation. It is involved in immune function, blood sugar control, steroid synthesis, reproduction, Parkinson's disease, epilepsy, backache, fatigue, depression and allergies.

It is found in red berries, oats, brown rice, whole wheat, vegetables, pulses, seafood, seeds and nuts.

CHROMIUM

I have not included this mineral in the tables which follow because we do not need much of it but it is absolutely essential in its role as a blood sugar regulator. It acts upon insulin that is required to stabilise blood sugar levels and so chromium is part of the mechanism for avoiding diabetes.

As a result of the action of chromium it is now seen as important in the slimming world. We only need about 50 mcg daily of dried matter. This can be found in apples, potatoes, tomatoes, eggs, peppers, orange juice and spinach in large enough quantities but it is found in general in vegetables, fruits and berries.

The effect of deficiency is normally diabetes.

SELENIUM

The requirement has been reduced for a variety of reasons from 150 mcg to 75 mcg daily although therapists in this field would still advise on 150 mcg daily.

It is a powerful antioxidant meaning it will help to protect the body from the destructive elements of toxins. It is particularly effective in protecting delicate structures such as cell membranes and it acts with Vitamin E. It helps to eliminate drugs and is important for most detoxification processes.

Deficiency can lead to cystic fibrosis, celiac disease, Crohn's disease, cataract, and alcoholism.

The best foods for selenium are cereals, nuts, seafood and liver. When wheat and rice are processed the destruction of selenium is almost total.

We need about 80 mcg daily and this is often hard to achieve so the best way of ensuring the correct balance of selenium is to eat liver, nuts, especially Brazil nuts, brown rice and pig's kidneys, or take a supplement.

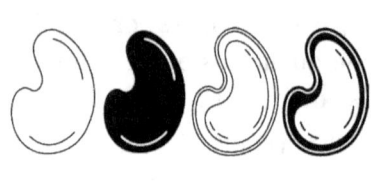
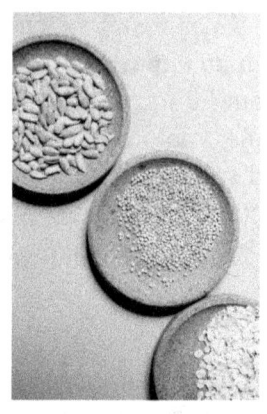

Other minerals that we need are molybdenum, iodine, silicon, and fluorine. We need miniscule quantities of boron, vanadium, tin, cobalt, nickel, sulphur and phosphates.

When you think about it, we are no more than a fabulous chemical refinery and there is more fascination to come. Just take a look at the world of vitamins!

VITAMINS

Recommended daily intake of Vitamins:

Vitamin A Retinol/Carotene: 1000 mcg.

Vitamin D: 10 mg.

Vitamin E: 15 mg.

Vitamin B1 Thiamine: This is linked to energy requirement so it is measured in mg per 1000 calories and an average intake is around 1.5 mg.

Vitamin B2 Nicotinamide: 10 mg from 60 gms of protein daily.

Vitamin B5 Pantothenic acid: 5 mg

Vitamin B6 Pyridoxine: 1.5 mg

Vitamin B12 Cyanocobalamin: 1.5 mcg

Folic acid: 300 mcg

Biotin: 40 mcg
Vitamin C: 1000 mg

VITAMIN A

Retinol is what we need but carotene is a precursor to retinol so the Vitamin A in vegetables and fruit, known as carotene is fine but it is good to have retinol too that does not exist in plant food.

Vitamin A is an antioxidant and it is therefore very important in the fight against infection and toxic damage. It helps in the battle to keep us well and free from illness.

We need six times more carotene than retinol but it could be provided by 4 ounces of carrots, so it is not hard to have the right amount of carotene, which converts to the right amount of retinol. 2 pounds of fresh vegetables will provide sufficient Vitamin A.

The best sources are cantaloupe melons, mangos, apricots, butter, cheddar cheese and red peppers, old carrots, spinach and endives.

But by far the highest levels are found in cod liver oil and liver in general.

VITAMIN C

This is one of the most important vitamins because it is so widely used by the body not only as a valuable antioxidant but also in so many enzymatic processes, which include complicated things such as processing steroids in the adrenal cortex and in converting cholesterol into bile acids.

A deficiency of this vitamin can lead to scurvy, which relates to a lack of strength in connective tissue such as our gums, listlessness and exhaustion, adrenal exhaustion, loss of appetite, high cholesterol levels, poor levels of immunity, increased risk of cancer, weakness in excreting toxic metals such as cadmium and lead, a reduction in anti-inflammatory activity and a reduction of the detoxification processes. It is an extremely important vitamin and we need about 1000 mg.

Vitamin C can be taken in enormous amounts without ill effects and in some cases of illness, up to 4 gms daily may be required.

It is found in liver and kidney but most other meats and fish contain almost none at all.

Apart from fruit and vegetables it is pointless looking for vitamin C so it is essential to eat plenty of these foods, the best being spring greens, parsley, broccoli, green and red peppers, blackcurrants and strawberries.

VITAMIN D

The most important role for this vitamin is to enable calcium to be absorbed through the intestine. It exists only in animal foods and these days when so many people work indoors and in offices where exposure to sunlight is limited, it is important that people have access to these sources of vitamin D. Those who have white skin and have sufficient exposure to sunlight will not be at risk.

Anyone deficient in this vitamin may be at risk of suffering from poor calcium absorption and therefore may experience the problems associated with calcium deficiency.

We need 1 mg daily if spending much of our time indoors and this is of particular interest to people running hospitals and nursing homes where patients have much less access to sunlight. But other vulnerable people include children, pregnant women and women who are breast-feeding.

We find the best vitamin D providers in eggs, butter, fish, cod liver oil, salmon, herrings, sardines and tuna.

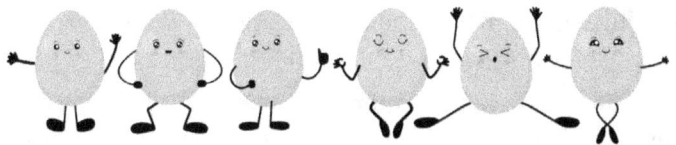

Clearly, the danger of taking too much would be the excess absorption of calcium leading to calcium dumping.

VITAMIN E

This is a particularly valuable vitamin because it lives in the membrane or skin of the cells and so it is able to do its job as an antioxidant right at the place where it is most needed. It is essential that we do not suffer from a deficiency of it.

Deficiency leads to infertility problems, weakened red blood cells, muscle weakness including the muscles of the heart and digestive tract. Deficiency also leads to damage of the nervous system and brain.

Premature babies are at risk of vitamin E deficiency.

Most of us are close to deficiency and the government thinks we only require about 6 mg daily but it is much safer to seek more like 10 mg.

If a person is in a job exposed to a lot of toxins such as a taxi driver, it is important to take at least 10 mg daily and more if possible. **Vitamin E is a crucial antioxidant.**[27]

Someone consuming a lot of junk food will be depleted but someone eating a lot of vegetables, grains, pulses, fruits and fish will have no difficulty reaching 18 mg.

High levels of vitamin E also have benefits such as keeping high blood pressure at bay, maintaining skin elasticity, preventing fibrocystic breast disease, improving mobility in arthritic patients and slowing the progress of Parkinson's disease.[27]

There are a huge number of diseases that benefit from the administration of Vitamin E at levels between 100–400 mg daily, but do not embark on additional vitamin E intake without speaking to an experienced nutritional practitioner.

Wheat germ provides more Vit E than anything else. Sadly, wheat germ is largely eliminated in the processing of wheat because of its unfavourable baking properties, as the oil is susceptible to oxidation which decreases shelf life.[28]

VITAMIN B1 THIAMINE[29]

This is an essential element in the production of energy and if it is deficient it will affect the nervous system more than any other part of the body.

We often associate our energy with our muscle capacity, and seldom do we think of the energy required by the brain, the nerves, the digestive system, the lymphatic system and so on. We need about 1 mg if we burn 2,000 calories daily. If we burn more calories, we need more thiamine.

Thiamine can be found in vegetables, pulses, nuts and seeds, fish, meat and wheat germ with the greatest source being, as usual, vegetables.

Severe deficiency leads to beriberi, which is not often seen and less severe deficiency leads to the possibility of lower levels of intelligence. A whole new debate on education lies herein! Alcohol levels may reduce our capacity to absorb thiamine which is cold comfort to most humans!

VITAMIN B2 RIBOFLAVIN

It is used as a co-factor in enzymatic processes that take place in the manufacture of energy or ATP. In this sense it is closely connected to thiamine. People who have low levels often suffer from heart disease, cancers, alcoholism, thyroid disease, and diabetes. The contraceptive pill and stress all increase riboflavin losses.

It is found in dairy produce, seafood, fish, vegetables, meats, fruit and pulses, with the highest levels in mushrooms.

We need around 1.5 mg daily and most people are able to access 2 mg daily without much trouble so there is little evidence of deficiency in this country except among junk food eaters.

VITAMIN B3 NIACIN

Like a number of other B vitamins, it is essential in the production of energy, and in very many other enzymatic activities. The amount required is no less than 10 mg daily and this can be obtained from about 60 gms of protein. It is better if these figures are raised slightly but most of us eat too much protein, so deficiency is not common.

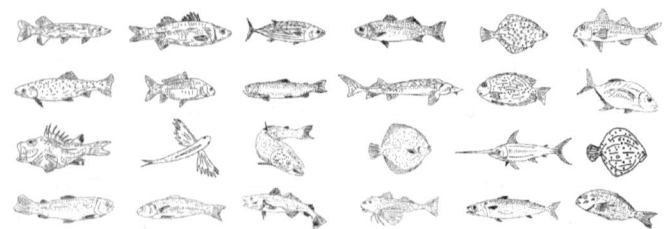

It is found in brown rice, anchovy, plums, and mushrooms and exists in particular in fish, vegetables, offal and pulses in general.

Deficiency leads to fatigue, indigestion, mental fatigue, apathy and insomnia.

VITAMIN B5 PANTOTHENIC ACID

It is required for energy production, cellular metabolism, synthesis of fatty acids, steroids, and it enables the cells to manage the protection, storage, transportation and relocation of proteins. We need close to 10 mg daily which is difficult but suggestions from scientists range from 2 mg to 25 mg so there is no agreement universally.

The best sources of this vitamin are parsley, broad beans, trout, chicken, endives and goat milk. In general we find it in vegetables, pulses, milk, and oats and fruit.

There are no known deficiency symptoms but it is rather obvious that due to its importance a deficiency will lead to fatigue and the ensuing problems related to cell degeneration.

VITAMIN B6

It is closely connected to the metabolism of nitrogen, which is produced by protein synthesis.

Proteins convert to amino acids and need this vitamin for the process. We need 1.05 mg daily if we consume 70 gms of protein but since most of us eat more protein than that, we need more B6, so we should be looking at 1.5 mg daily.

It is found mainly in fish, vegetables, pulses and nuts and seeds. It is especially abundant in leeks and trout. Severe deficiency is rare but is reflected in sleepiness, fatigue and anaemia.

VITAMIN B12

A deficiency of B12 may take a long time to appear but the symptoms include numbness to the hands and feet, unsteadiness, diminished position sense, moodiness, poor memory, confusion, agitation, depression, dim vision and delusions and seem to replicate senile dementia but respond well to vitamin B12 treatment.

If left untreated coronary heart disease can follow. If left untreated over a long period of time the myelin sheath that protects the nerves is inadequately formed and pernicious anaemia results.

The people at most risk from a deficiency are vegans because they do not eat any foods from animals and therefore are sometimes low in protein.

The best foods for B12 are lamb kidney, lamb liver, mussels and eggs. It is not found in plant foods at all. For those who do not like meat, mackerel is the best source.

FOLIC ACID

Chemotherapy cancer treatment sometimes uses a folic acid inhibitor because it slows down DNA synthesis and the idea is that if the levels of cell replication are slowed down, the new cancer cells will not develop so prolifically.

Folic acid is used in the synthesis of DNA and RNA. This is absolutely crucial to us. We need about 200 mcg daily to be on the safe side and we find it in lamb liver, black eye beans, endive and raspberries in particular, and vegetables, pulses and fruit in general.

It is difficult to be severely deficient unless following a junk food diet but deficiencies lead to oversized red blood cells known as megaloblastic anaemia. Deficiency affects cell division and therefore a child's growth can be affected. Cervical cancer can occur and the contraceptive pill appears to block the access of folate into some cells leading to the pre- cancerous condition known as cervical dysplasia.

Deficiency can lead to depression, gout, immune function weakness, osteoporosis, cardiovascular disease, birth defects and restless leg syndrome.

BIOTIN[30]

The cell just does not work efficiently without adequate supplies of biotin. It can be produced in the lower gut or colon, which means that a deficiency can arise if the colon is not functioning well.

It has a role in energy production not only from the citric cycle, but also from gluconeogenesis, a form of energy production from protein. It is used in fat metabolism. We need no less than 10 mcg daily although no figure has been set officially.

We find it in pulses, nuts, seafood, vegetables and fish.

SUMMARY

All this seems to be a bit academic but without these minerals and vitamins our body would not function properly. If we do not consume adequate supplies of these valuable and essential substances we will undoubtedly become ill and unable to function properly and slowly die.

Another interesting and valuable observation is the source of most of the vitamins and it cannot have passed unnoticed how important it is to **eat plenty of varied vegetables, fruits, pulses and fish.** Nuts and seeds too, are good sources of vitamins and minerals.

Grains such as brown rice and oats are also valuable. Of the meats, liver and kidneys are of greatest value.

It is for you to make choices about what you eat with a little more knowledge than you may have had at the beginning of this book. Whilst biochemistry is a very complicated science, you may now be able to create diets based upon some real and valuable facts and not upon the confusing array of information available at supermarkets and on all the packets and cans on display.

I find it fascinating that as a species we came from the earth and we eat plants which suck up the minerals and vitamins that exist in the earth and synthesise them to make them available for us to exist. Animals eat the plants too and we eat animals but our digestive system has to work twice as hard to extract the same nutrients that we get from plants with less effort. Animals are very tasty but do require more energy to digest.

Chapter 7

Good Foods

VEGETABLES

There are eight types of vegetables: leaf, root, stem, inflorescent, bulb, tuber, fruits which are often called vegetables and miscellaneous.

Fresh vegetables are full of moisture content and some, such as lettuce and celery, have less than 5% dry matter. The driest are garlic and sweet potato with 33% dry matter. This is good news for those trying to lose weight.

As a rule we need 500 gms daily of food dry matter, i.e. food with all the water extracted. To get this from vegetables alone would require an intake of nearly 6 kilogms! Our digestive system, unlike that of cows, could not possibly cope with that amount.

Another factor in regard to vegetables is their high fibre content with mustard and cress reaching almost 70% indigestible fibre.

Protein is not prevalent in vegetables. Someone consuming 1 kg of vegetables would be consuming 85 gms of dry solids that would yield 15 gms of protein.

Fat content is very low with an average of nearly 5% so 1 kg of vegetables would give only 4 gms of lipids (fat). **Great for slimmers!**

ENERGY IN VEGETABLES

Most vegetable energy comes in the form of carbohydrates, both sugar and starch. The average carbohydrate in all vegetables is 38%. The calorie content on average is 250 per 100 gms of dry matter. That means that if you could eat 2.5 kg of fresh vegetables a day, it would give you 212 gms of dry solids and your calorie intake would be 530. If you ate 1 kg of vegetables daily this would translate into 212 calories daily. You should remember that most people need no more than 2,100 calories daily so it is easy to see just how few calories of energy vegetables give us. It is difficult to add weight by eating a lot of vegetables so the question is *"where does excess weight come from?"* The answer is *"from carbohydrates"* which turn into sugar and unless burned off, is stored as fat. *Where do carbohydrates come from?* They come from bread, pasta, pizza bread, rolls, cakes, biscuits, sauce thickeners and all the myriad of processed foods that contain white flour. Also from cereals, whole rice, pulses, processed rice, potatoes and some root vegetables.

MINERALS AND NUTRIENTS IN VEGETABLES

We need minerals to function properly and we get plenty of these from vegetables in abundance. Average figures show that they give us only 170 mg of sodium and 3,000 mg of potassium per 100 g of solid matter. As previously explained, we need much more potassium than sodium so the benefits of vegetables are obvious. However, we must accept a wide variety of vegetables is required to gain this balance because our vegetables vary in their sodium and potassium content enormously. Too much sodium leads to acidosis so we need potassium to prevent that.

Calcium is very necessary in our diets and to this extent vegetables play an important role. On average they produce 551 mg per 100 g of dry matter so that our 1 kg of vegetables will give us 468 mg of calcium.

However, we must understand that at the same time as giving us high levels of calcium, vegetables must also give us high yields of magnesium and so we do need to mix our vegetables in order to give us a wide range of essential minerals. Something else we need to understand is that minerals sometimes work against each other as antagonists. For example, excess sodium will reduce potassium levels and high levels of calcium will reduce magnesium and zinc. Magnesium is an essential ingredient of the citric cycle that produces our energy. Zinc is an integral component of over 60 enzymatic activities and is especially important in the reproductive cycle so if we are overloaded with calcium these equally important minerals will become deficient leading to ill health. By eating a wide variety of vegetables we can avoid these problems.

TRACE MINERALS

Iron, zinc, manganese, copper, selenium, and chromium are all important trace minerals for our bodies and we get these from vegetables in particular. The vegetables, which are best able to give us these elements, are parsley, watercress, endive, asparagus, okra, lettuce, and mushrooms.

VITAMINS

There is no Vitamin A in vegetables but the precursor to it is found in yellow- and orange- coloured vegetables and is known as carotene. This acts as an antioxidant that helps the body to rid itself of toxins or waste products. Other coloured vegetables also contribute to carotene such as red peppers and greens. Our bodies convert carotene into Vitamin A.

There is no Vitamin D in vegetables. This is manufactured by the sun on our skin and is used to help us absorb calcium.

Vitamin E is sourced through vegetables. Vitamin E is an antioxidant.

The B vitamins are supplied in abundance by vegetables with mushrooms doing particularly well supported by onions, radishes, celery, endive lettuce, carrots, tomatoes, peppers, beans, peas, nuts, pulses, pumpkins, leeks, and mangetout.

Green leafy vegetables, green peppers, red peppers, and onions provide Vitamin C.

It can get very complicated to try to understand all the levels of vitamins that are supplied by the different vegetables so the best and easiest way is to enjoy as many vegetables as possible and know that you are consuming a variety of very important vitamins in the correct quantities. The problem some people have is eating only a selected few vegetables.

WHY ARE VEGETABLES SO IMPORTANT?

As I have said before, we are the sum of our cells. If we protect the cells in our body, we are effectively protecting ourselves. If a cell is unable to eliminate its toxins it will become damaged and its metabolic competence is weakened. This means it loses the capacity to support its DNA, its internal and external membranes or 'skin', its ability to synthesise proteins, especially its enzymatic proteins, its ability to produce ATP or energy, and its ability to eliminate toxins from inside itself which is called elimination and it is in this area that vegetables are essential. They provide the essential enzymatic co-factors to maintain the normal cell biochemistry. They provide potassium for maintaining the cell sap that the trace minerals and vitamins need as enzyme co-factors and a range of phytonutrients that protect the cells in a variety of ways. Phytonutrients that come from plants, fruit and vegetables are also powerful antioxidants, more so than Vitamin C or E.[31]

The cell that heals from free radical damage can turn its energies and resources to repairing older damage and ejecting the toxins that caused it. Phytonutrients have an immune stimulant activity, which protects the immune system. Vegetables, such as onions and garlic contain the biochemistry to offer detoxification activity.

Frankly, without vegetables in our diet, we will begin to suffer over a period of time from general ill health leading to chronic disease because our bodies will not be able to eliminate the toxins, which can ultimately kill us.

Measurements in g and mg

MARROW

Protein	2
Fats	0.8
Carbohydrates	8
Fibre	4
Minerals	***
Vitamins	***
Calories	44

KALE

Protein	2.3
Fats	1
Carbohydrates	1
Fibre	2.2
Minerals	***
Vitamins	***
Calories	22

High in manganese, Vitamin A, Vitamin E, B6, folate and Vitamin C

AUBERGINE

Protein	2
Fats	1
Carbohydrates	5
Fibre	2
Minerals	**
Vitamins	**
Calories	33

Quite a good source of magnesium, which is good for energy levels.

COURGETTE

Protein	4
Fats	1
Carbohydrates	4
Fibre	0
Minerals	***
Vitamins	***
Calories	42

PEPPERS

Protein	1
Fats	1
Carbohydrates	5
Fibre	2
Minerals	***
Vitamins	***
Calories	33

High in Vitamin A, especially the red ones. Good source of Vitamin E, B6.

TOMATO

Protein	1
Fats	0.2
Carbohydrates	4
Fibre	2
Minerals	***
Vitamins	***
Calories	25

RUNNER BEANS

Protein	2
Fats	0.4
Carbohydrates	4
Fibre	3
Minerals	***
Vitamins	***
Calories	25

High in folate, iron and magnesium.

LEEKS

Protein	2
Fats	0.7
Carbohydrates	4
Fibre	4
Minerals	**
Vitamins	**
Calories	31

Useful levels of Vitamin A, potassium, iron and manganese.

ONIONS

Protein	1
Fats	0.1
Carbohydrates	6
Fibre	1.2
Minerals	**
Vitamins	**
Calories	30

Contains quercetin, which is a strong antioxidant and is useful in its anti-cancer properties.

CAULIFLOWER

Protein	3.5
Fats	1
Carbohydrates	2
Fibre	1.6
Minerals	**
Vitamins	**
Calories	29

Good supply of potassium, magnesium and zinc.

SPROUTS

Protein	2
Fats	1
Carbohydrates	2.5
Fibre	2.4
Minerals	**
Vitamins	***
Calories	25

CABBAGE

Protein	1.6
Fats	0.3
Carbohydrates	2
Fibre	2.3
Minerals	***
Vitamins	**
Calories	20

LETTUCE

Protein	1.5
Fats	0.8
Carbohydrates	2
Fibre	2
Minerals	***
Vitamins	***
Calories	20

Lots of potassium and high levels of iron, phosphorous, with good levels of thiamine (B1), folate, biotin.

SPINACH

Protein	2.7
Fats	0.7
Carbohydrates	1.5
Fibre	3.4
Minerals	***
Vitamins	***
Calories	24

High in salt, potassium, calcium, iron, zinc and Vitamins A, E, niacin (B3) and folate.

WATERCRESS

Protein	1
Fats	0.2
Carbohydrates	0.1
Fibre	0.8
Minerals	***
Vitamins	***
Calories	6

This is an excellent source of minerals and vitamins but a lot must be eaten to take advantage of its fine properties which are calcium, salt, potassium, magnesium, iron, zinc, manganese, phosphorous and Vitamins A, E, and B6.

MUSHROOM

Protein	1.4
Fats	0.4
Carbohydrates	0.3
Fibre	2
Minerals	***
Vitamins	***
Calories	20

These are tremendous unless you are suffering from Candida but are full of riboflavin (B2), niacin (B3), B6, pantothenic (B5), biotin, potassium, copper, phosphorous, calcium and magnesium.

BEETROOT

Protein	1.5
Fats	0
Carbohydrates	7
Fibre	2.5
Minerals	**
Vitamins	*
Calories	33

Good for folate and a good ratio for calcium and magnesium.

CARROT

Protein	1
Fats	0.5
Carbohydrates	12
Fibre	3
Minerals	**
Vitamins	**
Calories	50

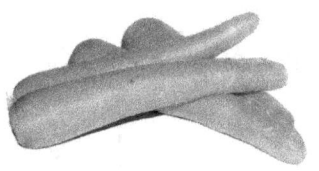

Plenty of Vitamin A.

CELERY

Protein	0.4
Fats	0.1
Carbohydrates	0.7
Fibre	1.2
Minerals	**
Vitamins	***
Calories	5

High in salt, potassium and iron.

POTATO

Protein	5
Fats	0.5
Carbohydrates	40
Fibre	3.5
Minerals	**
Vitamins	*
Calories	18

High in magnesium but not good in vitamins.

THE CASE FOR VEGETABLES

If you ate just a total of 1 kilogramme from an equal mix of 49 different vegetables it would contain the following:

IN GMS OF DRIED WEIGHT

Protein	17
Fat	5
Carbohydrates	37
Fibre	27
Calories	251

MINERALS IN GRAMS

Salt	170
Potassium	2980
Calcium	550
Magnesium	160
Iron	10
Zinc	3.5
Copper	0.6
Manganese	2.75
Phosphorous	450

VITAMINS IN MCG AND MG

Vit A	11 mg
Vit D	0
Vit E	6.5 mg
Vit C	330 mg
B1	1 mg
B2	0.5 mg
B3	6.5 mg
B5	7.5 mg
B6	1.5 mg
B12	0
Folate	614 mcg
Biotin	12 mcg

No one is going to eat a kilogramme of mixed vegetables and most certainly not an equal share of 49 of them but the point is that it demonstrates just how valuable vegetables are.

In the area of macro nutrients there is almost no fat, low protein, reasonable levels of carbohydrates and sufficient fibre but very low calories so, you might think that this is just OK, until we now look at the nutrient value of vegetables.

Vegetables contain low salt, high levels of potassium, magnesium, sufficient iron, high levels of zinc, manganese and calcium.

Vitamins are also in good supply with high levels of vitamins A, E, C, B1, B3, B5, B6, folate and the only minus points are zero vitamin D and B12 and low biotin levels. Overall, however, the mineral and vitamin content of vegetables is unsurpassed by any other food source so it is imperative to eat reasonable quantities of vegetables in order to supply the body with sufficient nutrients without which the body will not function properly.

A tip for those wishing to lose weight: the above selection of 49 vegetables, a whole kilogramme of them, will only add 251 calories to your diet.

A normal diet would probably contain more potatoes and possibly root vegetables, which would increase your weight and the carbohydrate levels and therefore your calories.

In contrast to the fresh vegetable table it is interesting to look at the next table that demonstrates the effects of processing some vegetables.

Collectively, a kilogramme of these three processed vegetables would give us rather weak returns.

BAKED BEANS
MUSHY PEAS
PROCESSED PEAS

Protein	20
Fats	3
Carbohydrates	55
Fibre	7
Minerals	*
Vitamins	*
Calories	250

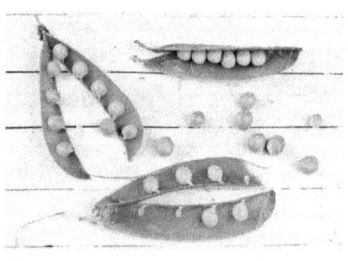

There are almost no vitamins in these three foods because the processing which involves heating destroys most of the vitamin value[32] and whilst the mineral values are not bad, the salt content is an enormous 1,000 mg which is almost our total daily allowance. The potassium value is too low being only 600 mg and magnesium is only 100 mg with iron returning only 7 mg and zinc only 3 with the remainder of the mineral values being very low indeed.

The calorie value is the same as for the kilo of vegetables but the danger is the very high salt content and although these products can sit on the shelf for years and still be used, why on earth would anyone want to eat a diminished food when the choice for something much better is so readily available.

The answer lies in the convenience of processed food but for the sake of your health I do not subscribe to the argument that everyone is too busy to cook or steam some vegetables or even to make gallons of superb vegetable soups.

PULSES, SEEDS, AND NUTS

COLLECTIVE NUTS ON AVERAGE

Protein	2.5
Fats	11
Carbohydrates	2.5
Fibre	2
Minerals	***
Vitamins	***
Calories	110

Excellent for magnesium, iron, and zinc and for Vitamin E although low in Vitamin A. Chestnuts are high in carbohydrates but low in fats and protein.

SEEDS

Protein	4
Fats	6
Carbohydrates	6
Fibre	0
Minerals	***
Vitamins	***
Calories	95

Similar in vitamin quality to nuts but excellent for iron and zinc. Sesame seeds are almost carbohydrate free but high in fats.

PULSES

Protein	24
Fats	2.8
Carbohydrates	51
Fibre	12
Minerals	***
Vitamins	***
Calories	300

Kidney, butter, broad, adzuki, black-eyed and mung beans, peas and lentils. *These are an excellent source of magnesium without too much calcium, and high in iron, zinc and copper. Similar to nuts and seeds for vitamin quality.* These foods are underestimated because they require quite a lot of preparation such as soaking overnight but this range of foods is very rewarding and can easily be used in soups and stews.

FRUIT

Fruit is very important in its role in the elimination process[33] but generally can eliminate more aggressively than vegetables. It is especially good for helping the cells excrete sodium, toxins and acidity. They promote elimination of toxins from the deepest levels but do nothing to assist stage 2 elimination where toxins are expelled from the superficial level to the outside via the organs of elimination such as the kidneys, liver, bowel and skin. If stage 1 of elimination is too strong, as when excess fruit is eaten, the sudden increase of sodium, toxins and acidity will produce unpleasant symptoms such as headaches as a result of these toxins circulating around the blood stream. Nevertheless, fruit for a healthy body is very important, as the body is always grateful for assistance with elimination, which is what fruit is best at. As a generalisation, fruit has low sodium, quite high potassium, and reasonable levels of calcium, magnesium and phosphorous, though it does not give such high levels as vegetables but it is necessary to eat both.

APPLES

Protein	0.6
Fats	0.1
Carbohydrates	20
Fibre	3.2
Minerals	*
Vitamins	***
Calories	75

Fruit in general is not terrific for providing us with minerals but good for vitamins. Apples give a helpful calcium to magnesium ratio, but no Vitamin D, E or B 12 and only low amounts of Vitamin A. It is a fine food though, especially for the liver.

BANANAS

Protein	2
Fats	0.4
Carbohydrates	37
Fibre	5
Minerals	**
Vitamins	***
Calories	150

High in potassium and excellent for magnesium.

ORANGES

Protein	1.7
Fats	0.1
Carbohydrates	13
Fibre	3
Minerals	*
Vitamins	***
Calories.	0

High in potassium.

FRUITS IN GENERAL

If an average of most of the available fruits in Europe is taken, the following data applies.

Protein	1.1
Fats	0.2
Carbohydrates	11
Fibre	3.8
Minerals	**
Vitamins	***
Calories	48

However, Bananas and grapes have the highest sugar content but a balance of 3 fruits a day should give us about 146 calories. It is not advisable to eat more than three pieces of fruit daily in order to keep the sugar content in check.

However, fruit gives us lots of potassium reducing the risk of acidity and it is low in salt. High levels of magnesium are offered which is good for our energy levels. Also of benefit are the high levels of iron and zinc but fruit gives us almost no vitamin D or B12. Fruit is good but vegetables are better!

FISH

Although high in protein fish also comes with considerable benefits. It is easier to digest and is high in polyunsaturated and essential fatty acids such as Omega 3 and Omega 6 oils. However, like all protein sources, it contains no fibre. The most beneficial fish are salmon, sardines, mackerel, eel, trout, herring and pilchards.

Eating oily fish has benefits such as:[34] Reducing the risk of clots, which can cause strokes and heart attacks. Reducing the risk of arterial disease. Lowering triglycerides (fats) in the blood by up to 65%. Reducing hypertension. Inhibiting the growth of tumours. Blocking inflammatory processes that encourage arthritis, cancer, psoriasis, diabetes and cell dysfunction.

Processed fish, like most other processed foods, is not to be encouraged so buy fresh fish and avoid salted or smoked fish. For best results steam it or boil it so that the goodness remains instead of being cooked out of it. Increasing amounts of fish are farmed and contain antibiotics so try to source unfarmed fish.

TROUT

Protein	36
Fats	11
Carbohydrates	0
Fibre	0
Minerals	***
Vitamins	***
Calories	259

Good for iron, zinc and magnesium. High in B1, B3, B6, B12 and B5.

SALMON

Protein	34
Fats	22
Carbohydrates	0
Fibre	0
Minerals	**
Vitamins	***
Calories	340

Good levels of magnesium, folate and Vitamin B5.

MACKEREL

Protein	37
Fats	31
Carbohydrates	0
Fibre	0
Minerals	**
Vitamins	***
Calories	433

Good magnesium, and high levels of Vitamin D, and B12.

COD

Protein	334
Fats	1.4
Carbohydrates	0
Fibre	0
Minerals	**
Vitamins	***
Calories	148

Good potassium, magnesium and Vitamin E.

ANCHOVY

Protein	26
Fats	6.3
Carbohydrates	0
Fibre	0
Minerals	**
Vitamins	***
Calories	171

High in iron, zinc and B3.

TUNA

Protein	37
Fats	6
Carbohydrates	0
Fibre	0
Minerals	***
Vitamins	***
Calories	176

Excellent for potassium, magnesium, iron and zinc. Most importantly, fish offers us retinol, one of the types of Vitamin A, which is hard to find elsewhere. It is also good for niacin (Vitamin B3).

FISH IN GENERAL

Protein	35
Fats	6.3
Carbohydrates	0
Fibre	0
Minerals	**
Vitamins	***
Calories	200

It is clear that fish gives us no fibre or carbohydrates but is nevertheless an important food that gives us high levels of magnesium, iron, zinc, plus vitamins B3, B5, B1, B6, B12 and biotin. It is disappointingly low in Vitamin C and E. Although herrings give us high levels of Vitamin D.

A diet high in vegetables, fruit and fish will give us most of the essential nutrients we need for a healthy life. Fish though are vulnerable to chemicals and plastics dumped into the sea so it is important to seek fresh local fish rather than imported fish and farmed fish and to cook it thoroughly.

SEAFOOD

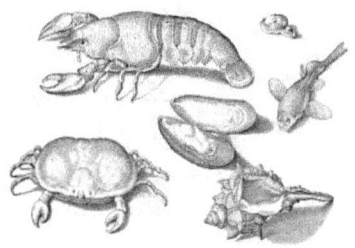

Generally, seafood is a wonderful source of minerals and vitamins but there are some dangers such as high levels of salt, and of course since these creatures are exposed more than most to heavy metal pollution from heavy industry, which sometimes dumps waste into waterways and the sea, it is unwise to eat large amounts of it. Nevertheless, seafood provides high levels of magnesium, iron and zinc: especially oysters. The reason why oysters are regarded as aphrodisiacs is because of the very high zinc content, which is regarded as essential for a healthy prostate gland, which in turn is associated with a healthy sexual performance. Whilst this is true, it is palpable nonsense to suggest that eating dozens of oysters on a regular basis will turn men into high performance Casanovas!

Seafood is also high in calcium, is good for protein, vitamins and minerals but has poor levels of Vitamin C and A. Finally, remember that prawns are high in cholesterol.

CRAB LOBSTER PRAWNS SHELLFISH

Protein	15
Fats	2
Carbohydrates	0
Fibre	0
Minerals	***
Vitamins	***
Calories	80

OFFAL IN GENERAL

Protein	25
Fats	8
Carbohydrates	0
Fibre	0
Minerals	***
Vitamins	***
Calories	175

Good for iron, zinc, copper and phosphorous. A good food.

KIDNEYS

Protein	24
Fats	4
Carbohydrates	0
Fibre	0
Minerals	***
Vitamins	***
Calories	132

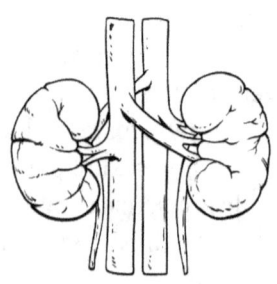

Excellent for B12, folate, iron, zinc, phosphorous but high in salt. A good occasional food.

LIVER

Protein	29
Fats	15
Carbohydrates	0
Fibre	0
Minerals	***
Vitamins	***
Calories	268

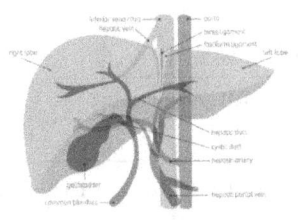

High in iron, zinc, copper, manganese, phosphorous and very good for retinol (Vitamin A), Vitamins D, B2, B3, B6, B12 and folate. Since our liver stores many minerals and vitamins it is a wonderful source of these nutrients but because of its role as a filter it can also bring to the table, as it were, toxins, which it also stores, so it should only be eaten about once per week.

CHICKEN AND GAME

(Pheasant, pigeon, guinea fowl, turkey etc)

Protein	30
Fats	6.5
Carbohydrates	0
Fibre	0
Minerals	***
Vitamins	***
Calories	179

No Vitamin A, D, C or B12 but good levels of B3, B6, folate, biotin and B5.

Please note that the levels of fat are low and that the corresponding calorie count is also low. Skinless chicken, assuming it is well reared and organic is a good food but it has no fibre.

CEREALS AND GRAINS/BROWN RICE AND MILLET

Protein	13 / 8
Fats	5 / 2
Carbohydrates	100 / 48
Fibre	7 / 7
Minerals	*
Vitamins	***
Calories	400 / 245

There is almost no salt and sugar in these foods, which means that they are slow to release carbohydrates from their starch content.

Their ratio of calcium to magnesium is a wonderful 1:10 and they are very high in zinc. These are much the best foods for achieving carbohydrates in your diet but cooking brown rice takes much longer than white rice.

Another benefit for those who are worried about their weight is the slim chance of adding unwanted pounds by eating brown rice or millet.

OATS

Protein	16
Fats	13
Carbohydrates	97
Fibre	10
Minerals	**
Vitamins	***
Calories	363

Good for minerals but with usefully low levels of salt, oats have an excellent calcium : magnesium ratio of 1:2 with high levels of iron, zinc, manganese and biotin but no Vitamin A, D, B12 and C.

Oats are a good source of energy especially when mixed with nuts seeds, sultanas, raisins, fruit and berries and makes an ideal breakfast and if some psyllium powder and wheat or oat bran is added it becomes a most satisfactory breakfast. Calories here are high which is no bad thing in the morning.

WHEAT GERM AND OAT BRAN

An excellent addition to breakfast cereal, it gives low levels of fat and the bran offers high fibre too but more significantly it offers low salt levels, high levels of magnesium, iron, zinc, manganese, phosphorous and copper and in general the levels of vitamins are high too except for Vitamins A, C, D and B12. It is a seriously good addition to oats and millet.

BUCKWHEAT, WHEAT FLOUR, PEARL BARLEY, RYE FLOUR

This group of grains are good for their mineral values but only average for vitamins. Excellent for magnesium, iron, zinc and manganese. However, the calories are high.

WHOLEMEAL WHEAT FLOUR

Protein	6
Fats	1
Carbohydrates	30
Fibre	4
Minerals	**
Vitamins	***
Calories	144

High levels of potassium and magnesium, good returns of zinc, manganese and phosphorous.

Chapter 8
Average Foods

DAIRY PRODUCTS

We were told to drink milk at school and it was free. The idea was to ensure that we did not contract rickets, a bone-wasting disease caused in part by a lack of calcium. This occurred after the war when rickets was a problem due to rationing of milk and fruit. However, if we had been instructed to eat more green leaf vegetables, our calcium intake would have been greater.

Raw milk was never a bad food in moderate quantities as it contains much that is good but it has to be remembered that it was designed for calves and NOT humans; so why it is held in such high esteem as a good food for humans is odd. Breast milk is especially designed for babies. It alters as the baby grows older because the changes are designed for the baby's changing digestive requirements.[35]

Eventually the baby is weaned off mother's milk onto solids just as calves are weaned off cow's milk and onto grass.

Cow's milk has large molecules digestible by calves but too large for babies and is often the cause of allergies in babies. It really is not a food suitable for babies and with all the processing that is associated with milk production is not particularly suitable for adults either. Nearly all milk has been processed thereby altering the original product.

Pasteurisation

Heated to 60 degrees for 30 minutes or 72 degrees for 15 seconds, the dangerous bacteria are destroyed along with the beneficial bacteria. Most of the natural enzymes are also destroyed.

Sterilisation

All the organisms are destroyed, good and bad.

Homogenised

The fat droplets are broken up so that the skimmed milk and cream no longer separate. The fat is easier to digest. This is good for commercial purposes.

Skimmed

There is less saturated fat, which is good. However, there is no vitamin A or D and the disadvantages of milk are still present.

Cream

Single cream has about 18% fat and double cream has 48%. Clotted cream has 60%.

Butter

This is 100% saturated fat.

Cheese

A milk concentrate with added salt: up to 1,400 mg per 100 gms. Heavy cheese eating will disrupt the sodium/potassium balance.

Cheese production releases free enzymes, which convert to toxins in many people.

Tyramine for example often leads to headaches.

Whey

Used as a food additive it is found in many processed foods such as soups, margarine and packaged cereals such as Muesli.

Cottage cheese

It is made from skimmed milk with added organisms producing lactic acid, carbon dioxide, citric acid and ethyl alcohol. Cream is often added.

Yoghurt

Lower in lactose (the name for sugar in milk) than milk, reducing allergy formation but most yoghurt is made from cow's milk with all the disadvantages. Many types of yoghurt have cream or dried skimmed milk added.

Evaporated and condensed milk

About a third of water is removed and sugar is added.

Casein

Milk protein, which is separated out for use in manufactured food products. It is found as a glue-like binding agent in a vast range of processed foods including burgers, sausages, pies and so on.

THE DANGERS OF MILK

All pre-processed milk contains lactic acid, which aids digestion. In all the milk we consume, whether as milk, cheese or in processed foods, the lactic acid has been destroyed in pasteurisation making it very hard to digest although boiling it aids digestion.[36]

Additionally, pasteurisation destroys 50% of Vitamin C and 25% of the B group vitamins.

Antibiotics are destroyed by pasteurisation enabling undesirable milk bacteria to multiply.

Experiments on cats, rats and calves have shown very detrimental effects after being fed on pasteurised milk but none when fed on raw unprocessed milk. Unprocessed milk is a good food if sourced in hygienic conditions but loses its goodness during processing.

Sodium

Milk encourages sodium to enter the cells of the body leading eventually to a dangerous imbalance of the sodium:potassium ratio and to acidity. Sodium in the cell leads to:

Depletion of energy.

Calcium and magnesium imbalance.

Accumulation of toxins in the cells and tissues.

Acidity and mucus production

Poor fluid handling

Susceptibility to and worsening of chronic illness.

Osteoporosis rarely exists among populations who do not consume large amounts of dairy produce. Although things are changing, Japan once had very few cases of arthritic diseases and osteoporosis due in no small part to the fact that calcium levels were kept lower than in Western countries where milk is so popular. This meant that the Japanese consumed less calcium and therefore avoided the problems associated with calcium dumping.

In Britain it is an increasing problem regardless of the fact that most people think that by drinking milk their bones will resist osteoporosis.[37]

Magnesium is essential for regulating calcium metabolism but dairy produce depletes magnesium and its ratio is about 10:1 in favour of calcium. The ratio should be closer to 4:1.

DETRIMENTAL EFFECTS OF EXCESS DAIRY CONSUMPTION

Dairy protein can lead to acid in the tissues of the body. When this happens, calcium, which is an alkaline mineral, is taken from the bones to reduce the acidity in the tissues. As this begins to occur the body produces more oestrogen because this is the hormone that enables calcium to combine with other substances to make bone.

When there is a threat of calcium loss from bone the body ensures that more oestrogen is manufactured. This is why so many menopausal women are recommended to take HRT.

The liver then makes more cholesterol because oestrogen depends on cholesterol and this can be a threat because high cholesterol levels in the blood can lead to heart and circulation problems.

Additionally, calcium is absorbed through the gut more effectively when its ratio with phosphorous favours calcium. Excess phosphorous, from milk consumption, draws out calcium from our bones and binds with it in the gut creating a ratio which favours phosphorous, which leads to poor calcium absorption and calcium depletion.

Thus dairy products, although high in calcium, are also high in phosphorous, creating poor absorption of calcium and ironically possible calcium deficiency.

What all this means is that people who consume a lot of milk, cheese and dairy produce, put themselves at risk by altering the balance of magnesium in the cells leading to fatigue and cell damage. Furthermore, there is a greater risk of calcium being drawn from bone leading to bone diseases and this in turn leads to excess cholesterol manufacture, which can lead to heart and circulatory problems. High sodium levels can lead to high blood pressure and excess calcium in cells can lead to the malfunction of cells, including a hardening of cells, which can lead to a sense of tension, stress, and muscle stiffening.

As we know, many farmers add growth hormones to cows' feed; so drinking milk will include consuming more growth hormones than is good for us. Bovine growth hormones are not destroyed in the processing of milk so they are able to affect humans.

Western populations are growing larger, particularly in America and Holland when compared to other countries that consume less milk.

Perhaps this has something to do with the extraordinary development of young children who often appear to be so adult in their appearance but, while their bodies seem to be so mature, I wonder if their brains are as developed.

There are many studies that show irrefutable evidence that milk consumption is sometimes associated with:[38]

Cardiovascular diseases. Diseases of the digestive tract. Poor absorption of nutrients. Excessive mucous production. Allergies. Asthma. Eczema. Cancer. Arthritis. MS, chronic fatigue syndrome and Immune system deficiencies.

Recommendation

Do your best to reduce all milk consumption, cheese and cows' milk yoghurt.

Alternatives may not be palatable initially but you will eventually begin to enjoy soya milk (no added salt or calcium or sugar) or even oat milk and rice milk. Goat's milk has less salt, sugar and calcium and is easier to digest.

Do not, in most cases, feed infants on cows' milk. Many problems may arise in future years. 25% go on to develop allergies, infections or atherosclerosis.

If someone has 3 bowls of cereal a week, 20 cups of tea and 7 cups of coffee all with milk, they will consume about 2,000 gms weekly and 300 gms daily. But this does not include any cheese.

COWS' MILK – SKIMMED

Protein	9
Fats	0.3
Carbohydrates	14
Fibre	0
Minerals	***
Vitamins	*
Calories	90

There is no fibre in milk and no starch. Nor are there any Vitamins E, D or carotene. It is good for retinol, one form of Vitamin A, and for B12 and biotin. It has high quantities of salt, calcium, zinc and phosphorous.

SEMI-SKIMMED

Protein	8
Fats	4
Carbohydrates	12
Fibre	0
Minerals	***
Vitamins	*
Calories	110

Similar to skimmed milk.

WHOLE MILK

Protein	6.5
Fats	8
Carbohydrates	10
Fibre	0
Minerals	***
Vitamins	*
Calories	135

Excellent source of retinol and zinc.

HUMAN MILK

Protein	6
Fats	7
Carbohydrates	20
Fibre	0
Minerals	***
Vitamins	**
Calories	135

Very high levels of retinol (Vitamin A), Vitamin E and no B6 or biotin but a lot of Vitamin C.

YOGHURT

Protein	11
Fats	6
Carbohydrates	15
Fibre	0
Minerals	***
Vitamins	*
Calories	156

Lots of folate and good for zinc and phosphorous.

HARD CHEESE

Protein	27
Fats	32
Carbohydrates	0
Fibre	0
Minerals	***
Vitamins	*
Calories	384

Very high levels of salt and disappointing levels of potassium making it an acid generating food. There is no Vitamin C and although it has high levels of zinc and phosphorous, it has a seriously poor ratio of calcium to magnesium (20:1) which impacts upon the body's calcium metabolism. It is this fact that makes it a suppressive food meaning that it suppresses the manufacture of energy. Furthermore, it has strong allergy forming properties so asthma sufferers beware.

SOFT CHEESE

Protein	18
Fats	16
Carbohydrates	1
Fibre	0
Minerals	***
Vitamins	*
Calories	200

High in salt, low in potassium, but good for zinc and phosphorous. Compare the difference between hard and soft cheese and imagine how salty a piece of Stilton tastes. It may come as a surprise that hard cheese is much higher in salt content than soft cheese.

The biggest problem with cheese is its salt content and salty foods become a habit, which explains why food manufacturers use so much of it.

GOATS' MILK

Protein	7
Fats	7
Carbohydrates	10
Fibre	0
Minerals	***
Vitamins	**
Calories	135

Much more potassium than salt and it has very high levels of magnesium compared to its calcium levels making it a much safer milk to drink.

SHEEP'S MILK

Protein	8
Fats	9
Carbohydrates	7
Fibre	0
Minerals	***
Vitamins	*
Calories	139

Lots of zinc.

SOYA MILK

Protein	6
Fats	4
Carbohydrates	1.5
Fibre	0
Minerals	***
Vitamins	**
Calories	60

SOYBEAN

It has a ratio of 1:3 in favour of potassium; 1:1.4 in favour of magnesium over calcium and it is good for folate, riboflavin, Vitamin E and iron. And just look at the low levels of calorie output. Good for slimmers! But I now wonder how much deforestation occurs to produce Soya?

EGGS

Protein	8
Fats	7
Carbohydrates	0
Fibre	0
Minerals	***
Vitamins	***
Calories	94

Equal levels of salt and potassium but five times more calcium than magnesium. It is good for iron and zinc with high levels of retinol, lots of Vitamin D, Vitamin E and B12 with excellent levels of biotin and pantothenic acid (B5). Avoid raw eggs because they contain high levels of cholesterol.

BUTTER

Protein	0.2
Fats	38
Carbohydrates	0
Fibre	0
Minerals	*
Vitamins	*
Calories	348

High levels of retinol but a ratio of 50:1 in favour of salt over potassium and almost no minerals at all but delicious for all that!

In spite of its emptiness as a food it is much tastier than margarine but if bread and roll consumption is really low, as I recommend it should be, the small amount of butter spread on the bread will not be too detrimental so long as there is a good core diet to offset its dangers.

PROCESSED GRAINS AND CEREALS

WHITE RICE / BROWN RICE

Protein	+6%
Fats	+25%
Carbohydrates	+2.5%
Fibre	-31%
Minerals	*
Vitamins	*
Calories	+4%

These figures show the percentage differences of white rice from brown rice due to processing

The processing of rice gives us higher levels of protein, fat and carbohydrates but much less fibre and more seriously the processing destroys 30% of salt, 42% potassium, 400% calcium, 72% magnesium, 65% iron, 2.8% zinc, 93% copper, 91% manganese and 83% phosphorous. Minerals are very diminished. Vitamins are nearly as denuded too with an 87% loss of Vitamin E, 32% thiamine (B1), 72% riboflavin (B2), 22% niacin (B3), and 60% folate.

It is not difficult to see just how much goodness is lost when food is processed.

CORNFLAKES

Protein	3
Fats	0.3
Carbohydrates	33
Fibre	1.3
Minerals	**
Vitamins	*
Calories	140

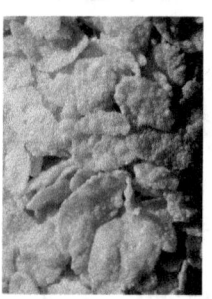

No Vitamins A or C, and very high levels of salt and iron.

FROSTIES

Protein	2
Fats	0.2
Carbohydrates	36
Fibre	0.5
Minerals	***
Vitamins	*
Calories	147

Very low levels of potassium but high levels of salt and iron.

SHREDDED WHEAT

Protein	4
Fats	1
Carbohydrates	28
Fibre	4
Minerals	**
Vitamins	*
Calories	133

Good levels of magnesium and iron.

WEETABIX

Protein	4
Fats	1
Carbohydrates	28
Fibre	4
Minerals	**
Vitamins	*
Calories	133

Good levels of magnesium and iron.

The problem with processed cereals is that they tend to contain high levels of salt. Salt is a preservative and keeps the cereal crisp but although some minerals are in good supply the vitamin levels are not good and the energy levels from them are not nearly as efficient as oats. One small piece of unprocessed maize contains almost no salt at all but the processing of it adds 3,000% more salt without which the flake will be soggy and it will not last a long time in the box.

Many cereals contain lots of sugar and chemicals to make them last longer on the shelves and once again I return to the theme of empty foods which give us only small amounts of energy.

THE PROCESSING OF WHITE FLOUR

All wheat has to be ground, but whole meal wheat is produced by grinding the whole grain, the germ, which contains all the nutrients, the husk, or outer skin which contains all the fibre and the gluten containing all the energy.[39]

Processing the ground wheat takes the germ and fibre content out of the flour leaving just the grey gluten, which needs to be dyed white and added chemicals to fluff it up.

The losses to processing are dramatic: Vitamin E 78%, thiamine 32%, riboflavin 66%, niacin 64%, B6 70%, folate 45%, pantothenic 62%, biotin 85%.

The minerals fare no better: Potassium 60%, calcium 268%, magnesium 74%, zinc 69%, copper 60%, manganese 77% and phosphorous 64%.

This is just an example of how seriously processing foods affects what we eat.

The bulk nutrients such as protein and fats are not as affected but the tiny amounts of micro nutrients which are every bit as important are very seriously eroded and so I make this plea for everyone to avoid processed foods as much as is possible. They are empty foods and often you will see that they are fortified with added vitamins or minerals to meet the government's requirement.

Why does the food industry take out the good things from many foods but is then required to replenish them? It is because the processing of foods makes for easier storage, transport and packaging and with added colourings and flavourings it can appear to be appetising which can lead to higher profits. It staggers me that nearly 7/8ths of all available supermarket foods are packaged, frozen, pre-cooked, canned and displayed with attractive packaging to tempt the buyer into thinking that it is the real deal.

Wheat is the most common of the cereals and makes up about 30% of USA diets.[40] The most common problem concerning wheat is in the process of milling. Most of the goodness of wheat lies in its bran or fibre and in its germ. The largest part of a grain of wheat contains gluten and this is the least nutritional part. It is a glue-like substance and is found in a vast array of processed foods such as a thickening agent so it is in most sauces, breads, biscuits, cakes, cereals, pasta, pizza, pastries, pasties and also beers, lagers and other alcoholic drinks.

It is very difficult indeed to have a wheat free diet. Most of the nutrient-rich parts of wheat are discarded because it is more beneficial to sell a processed and deficient product to a gullible public for the sake of easy milling and good profits. The reasons that make separation of the flour components attractive are:

Easy bulk handling of white flour.

Good storage qualities of white flour.

The public likes the appearance and texture of white bread. But white flour has comparatively low nutritional value. Look at the following tables.

WHOLEMEAL FLOUR

Protein	14.77
Fats	2.56
Carbohydrates	74.32
Fibre	10
Energy	360

WHITE FLOUR

Protein	13.37
Fats	1.63
Carbohydrates	87.57
Fibre	4
Energy	396

PROCESS LOSS %

Protein	9.45
Fats	36.36
Carbohydrates	-17.84
Fibre	57
Energy	-10

White flour produces less protein, fat and fibre but more carbohydrate and energy. Unless you are very active it will make you gain weight but at the same time it will give you less nutrition, vitamins and minerals and much less fibre giving rise to an increased appetite.

ESSENTIAL MINERALS IN BREAD

	Whole	Processed	% Loss
Manganese	3.61	0.81	74
Phosphorous	372	140	62.5
Sodium	3	3	0
Potassium	395	151	62
Magnesium	140	36	74
Iron	4.5	2.4	69
Zinc	3.4	1	69

All these minerals are essential for the body to function normally so the mineral losses and gains are significant, especially for people who eat a lot of white bread, pasties, biscuits, pasta, pizzas, sauces, burgers, sausages, cakes, rolls and so on and so on.

Essential vitamins

There are mixed reviews on this topic but on average the production of white flour loses 67% of valuable vitamins.

White flour produces more energy from more carbohydrate because it turns to sugar but has much less fibre, protein and 'useful' fat.

Apart from much higher levels of calcium, which can become a problem, it is deficient in all minerals and vitamins.

So why do we prefer it to whole meal bread? Is it texture, colour, durability and availability or have we never tried the alternatives?

And what are the problems with gluten? Well, it takes forever for the digestive system to process and it is made up of proteins called gliadins and glutelins. These are:

Hard to digest.

They exert a toxic effect upon the immune system They have poor nutritional value.

Further problems surrounding white flour

It is bleached for appearance and some of the bleaching chlorines are left in the flour.[41]

It seems that very white bread is more popular than 'good' bread despite the dangers that lie in the processing.

Viv Richards, a famous West Indies cricketer, used to suffer miserably from hay fever, streaming nose and watering sore eyes until he was advised to avoid white bread. His allergy ceased and he continued unhampered by eating whole meal bread instead.

Bread, especially white bread, has allergy forming properties and it is made from white flour so all white flour products have the same effect, so when we talk about white bread, we also include pastas, pizza, rolls, pita bread and so on. It has a detrimental effect upon our digestion and those who suffer from a sluggish digestive system with bloating should give up eating bread for a month and experience the difference.

But **beware**! Brown bread is, very often, white bread dyed brown. Sometimes 'granary bread' is white bread (bleached) with added colouring (brown) plus a few whole grains thrown in to make it healthy. Try and stick to 100% whole meal bread even though it is almost impossible to find in the conventional shops. Commercial whole meal bread has a little whole meal flour but is still made from white flour (80%).

Commercial bread is heavily salted and will upset the sodium/potassium balance if eaten in abundance. It contains yeast that can encourage candida in the intestine. Additional fat too, is unhelpful.

Fibre is lacking and fibre is vital for a sound digestive system to avoid constipation and for helping to reduce dangerous cholesterol levels in the blood. Furthermore, the gluey consistency of gluten can lead to a sluggish and glutinous mucus lining of the gut, which prevents effective digestion.

Some of the adverse factors of wheat consumption

There is a possible connection between wheat and arterial disease.

There is a connection between wheat and 'Baker's Asthma'.

Celiac patients, those allergic to gluten, are at far greater risk from lymphatic cancer. Dermatitis is often associated with wheat intolerance.

Wheat proteins often depress the immune system, which protects us from disease. Mouth ulcers can be attributed to high wheat intake.

Sufferers of IBS respond positively (15–71%) from the elimination of wheat, milk and eggs.

Because of the impact that wheat can have upon the immune system, asthma sufferers often find relief once wheat has been eliminated from their diet.

Suggestions

Bearing in mind the prevalence of wheat in our diet, it is sensible to:

Reduce bread eating.

Eat only whole meal bread where at all possible.

Don't eat pasta, white rice and bread on the same day.

Switch carbohydrate consumption to oats, brown rice, potatoes or millet. Try and avoid processed wheat (simple carbohydrate) and seek only complex carbohydrates: brown rice, oats, maize, whole meal bread or millet.

Don't forget that wheat is also in pasta, pizza, pastry, cakes and biscuits and all manner of gravy-making foods such as Oxo cubes or granules.

MEAT

As a generalisation, non-meat eaters who also avoid dairy products are less likely to suffer from cancer, heart disease, and osteoporosis and usually have lower blood pressure.[42]

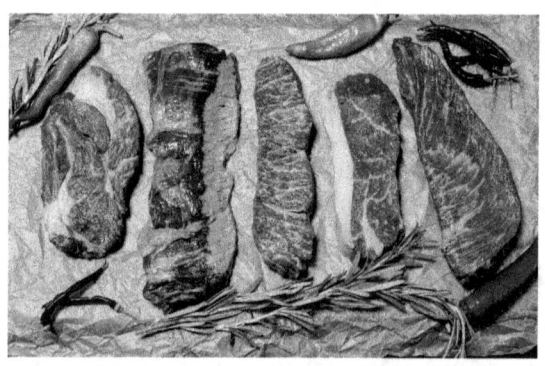

THE PROBLEMS WITH MEAT

Even a succulent fillet steak is as 'tough as old boots' for the digestive system and therefore requires more energy to digest it.

This energy could be used to detoxify the body but is being used to digest meat so there is less energy for the elimination of toxins. It makes meat a suppressive food.

Meat contains high levels of protein. Diets high in protein are more likely to be linked to diseases because excess protein breaks down into ammonia before breaking down again into uric acid, each of which are toxic. Fat in meat is also a commonly known problem.

Daily consumers of meat have been shown to have a higher risk of developing lung cancer in men and breast cancer in women.

Meat produces ammonia in the gut which can lead to putrefaction (rotting) and this encourages unfriendly bacteria, which exude toxins into the blood stream and liver and can lead to diseases of the colon.

Meat often contains toxins from the use of modern farming practices. These include the use of hormones, antibiotics, herbicides and pesticides. Studies have shown that bovine growth hormones can lead to prostate, bladder and testicular cancers in humans.

Animals are given antibiotics to control their susceptibility to disease leading to an inability in human meat eaters to control the fungus, Candida Albicans. Candida is not bacteria and is not killed by antibiotics, it is a fungus. A steady intake of antibiotics destroys good bacteria in the gut leading to the growth of Candida. Some meats, such as game, are unaffected by hormones and antibiotics because they are not usually reared in mass.

Meat contains high levels of saturated fats. In the past this amounted to about 4% but due to modern farming techniques for greater profit, the fat content is closer to 30%. This means that the value of meat has been eroded and lean meat is being replaced by fatty meat. Much cheaper to produce but not necessarily cheaper to buy!

Frying, grilling and barbecuing meat creates dangerous substances in the meat, which may damage DNA causing cancers and heart disease.

Beef 30–50% saturated fat – very hard to digest.

Pork 35–60% saturated fat – Very suppressive and high in salt.

Lamb 30–45% saturated fat – Less toxic and easier to digest.

Horsemeat, Venison, Ostrich, Wild Boar etc. – In general the more intense the farming, the more likely the contamination of food. Horse, deer, wild boar and so on are not reared on a mass scale so their meat may be of a better quality but eating is a subjective thing so horsemeat and venison have its detractors.

Of far greater concern is the quantity of largely undeclared 'additions' – lips, ears, connective tissue, antibiotics, growth hormones – that go into food and the misleading and confusing information that accompanies it.

Poultry 20–25% saturated fat – Easier to digest. Less farmed out.

Game Less contaminated – Lots of iron. Easy to digest.

Offal – Full of vitamins and minerals but can also contain a lot of toxins.

Other meat products

These foods are made up from wastes of other meats. Meat left on the bone is mechanically stripped and often contains tendons and cartilage.

Lips and ears are ground up and used in burgers and sausages, pies, faggots, frankfurters, paté and black pudding.

Additives are used to make meat leftovers more desirable, such as:

Rusk derived from white wheat flour

Soya flour or soya proteins

Milk derivatives

Salt

Yeast extract

Monosodium glutamate

Sodium nitrate

Added fat

Vegetarian burgers suffer the same fate.

The food industry wastes nothing in its processing, so rest assured that although the meat product, burger, pasty, pie, scotch egg etc. is so tempting and tasty, it is given such a makeover that it is easy to fall for its appearance, taste and the sheer joy of eating it, but, and seriously but, it is of little value to the body and is a downright dreadful, dare I call it, food! Enjoy it very occasionally as a treat but not as part of a staple diet.

MEAT VALUES

Assuming that the amount of meat is 150 gms:

BEEF

Protein	27
Fats	18
Carbohydrates	0
Fibre	0
Minerals	**
Vitamins	**
Calories	329

Good for Magnesium, Potassium, Iron and Zinc, but an absence of Vitamin A, E, D, C and biotin.

Sufficient B2, B12 and B6 and very good B3.

Sirloin has the lowest protein but the highest fat content. Stewing steak has the highest protein and lowest fat content.

But just compare these figures with those for any vegetable and you will notice just how much more protein and fat the meat gives but with no fibre and no carbohydrates.

LAMB

Protein	23
Fats	43
Carbohydrates	0
Fibre	0
Minerals	**
Vitamins	**
Calories	488

Breast, chops, cutlets, leg, scrag, neck and shoulder.

No Vitamin A, C, D, and low E but good B3, and B12. Chops have the lowest levels of protein and the highest fat and the highest calories but leg has the lowest fat. The calories in meats come from their fat content since there are no carbohydrates.

PORK

Protein	23
Fats	42
Carbohydrates	0
Fibre	0
Minerals	**
Vitamins	**
Calories	481

Belly, chops and legs. *Good for B1, B12, but no Vitamin A, D, or C.*

MEAT IN GENERAL

Protein	27
Fats	25
Carbohydrates	0
Fibre	0
Minerals	**
Vitamins	**
Calories	340

Good for niacin (B3), riboflavin (B2), B6, B12, folate, pantothenic (B5), and biotin, but no carbohydrates or fibre.

Chapter 9

Poor Foods

HOW ARE FOODS PROCESSED?

Much has been written about how various forms of cooking can destroy the goodness in food. As a generalisation raw or natural food has not had its nutrients and minerals cooked out of it but it is not always practical to eat raw food. Nevertheless, we should be aware that cooking involves heating and this alters and reduces the nutritional and mineral value of food. It is quite obvious to most people that a fresh apple has more goodness in it than a cooked one; a raw tomato has more goodness than a cooked one. However, much of our food requires cooking.

Processed foods have been created for convenience, storage, transport, appearance and profit.

Canning

Considerable loss of soluble nutrients (vitamins and minerals). Added salt, sugar or vegetable oil. Canning peas increases salt content by 230%, losses of over 60% of potassium, 50% of magnesium and 60% of vitamin B.

Freezing

This is not such a depleting process but most fruits and vegetables are blanched before freezing and lose much of their goodness in the heating.

Drying

The detrimental effects of this form of processing are similar to canning with added depletion of Vitamin C.

Salting

In some cases, the salt content in salted food such as bacon is colossal.

Smoking

Often used with salting e.g. smoked salmon, haddock and bacon. Smoking produces benzopyrene which some regard as a cancer-forming chemical.

Sugar

Used for preserving jams, the sugar content is usually enormous. The sugar has been refined and is of no nutritional value at all, but does carry high calories. Furthermore, the nutritional value of the fruit in jams has been diminished to almost negligible levels through cooking.

Separation

Many processed foods have had oils, fats or moisture removed because their presence would lead to the parent food becoming rancid. The process of separation often affects other nutrients and minerals of value to the detriment of the consumer.

Chemical preservatives

There are approximately 35 permitted preservatives in this country but they do not include vinegar, alcohol, salt, sugars, antioxidants, artificial sweeteners, bleaching agents, emulsifiers, improving agents, additives, or stabilisers. They are numbered 200–293. No one really knows the effects upon humans if consumed regularly for 50 years.

Irradiation of food including microwaving

A fairly recent innovation, no one knows the long-term effects upon humans but animal experiments show:

Growth rates are slowed

Muscle tissue breakdown

Increased tumours

Blood clotting problems

Heart lesions

Kidney damage

Fewer and smaller offspring

Miscarriages

Mutations in offspring

Testicle and sperm damage

It has been proven that vitamins in particular are adversely affected and reduced.

Additives

There are six groups and one of them includes artificial additives. The body lacks the enzymes to deal with these and eliminate them so they remain in the cell and hinder its processes hence they must be regarded as a toxin.

There are roughly 54 different emulsifiers and stabilisers in the E 400 category. 50 colourings are permitted but the 4 'intense' sweeteners allowed in the UK are disallowed in the E.U. There are a further 100 additives allowed by law. Included is monosodium glutamate, which is not allowed in baby foods.

Disadvantage of additives

Increased toxicity, allergy and intolerance. These are mainly unnatural substances, which the body is unaccustomed to and no one knows what the long-term effect is upon humans.

Food packaging

Chlorinated hydrocarbons are used in the plastics industry, which possess special toxicity to both the liver and kidneys. They have been implicated in 'chemical acne' induced in Japanese and Taiwanese populations who ingested rice oil contaminated with these toxins. There is a disturbing notion that there is an association between plastic packaging and male infertility. There is no knowledge of the long-term effects upon human beings. As we now know, plastics are hazardous to sea creatures and to us humans.

Dried and smoked foods

Polycyclic hydrocarbons and sulphur dioxide can result from partial combustion such as on a barbecue. Smoked fish and dried foods such as fruit and tea are at risk of being contaminated with these chemicals, which contain the notorious carcinogen (cancer-forming toxin) benzopyrene.

Plastic containers

Plasticisers are used to give containers a finished look. Much of this kind of plastic is used increasingly for storage of food and drink, e.g. the milk bottle. Once upon a time there was a real danger from lead pipes. The lead would 'leach' into the water and poison people. Today the problem with plastic packaging and containers is that their chemicals also leach into the food or drink that they contain.

It is much better to store food and drink in glass or stainless-steel containers.

Medical drugs

The side effects of medical drugs are well known in general, but we are told that they are not as bad as the illness that the drugs are supposed to cure. Nevertheless, far too many medical drugs have very unpleasant side effects, which are sometimes the cause of death rather than the disease that they are supposed to cure.

Antibiotics, which are used extensively in the food industry, and Paracetamol are two well-known drugs that are poisonous to the liver.

It is wise to check for the side effects of drugs before using them.

Contaminants in water supply

Chlorine is used in our water supply to kill off bacteria. It is important that the unwanted bacteria are treated but it is equally important that the chlorine is thoroughly eliminated but this is not done unless a filter system is in place in the home.

Chlorine, agrochemicals and oestrogen (from the use of the fertility pill) are all evident in drinking water. These are dangerous to our health.

It is incumbent upon us to do what the water companies do not do and that is to filter our drinking water completely.

Animal hormones

Many farm livestock are fed with growth hormones for bulking, and antibiotics to keep disease at bay. These chemicals find their way into the food chain either through the meat that is provided or through our drinking water.

These drugs are especially present in meats and milk. It is advisable to choose, where possible, organic meat and milk because no one knows what the results are of eating food that is contaminated with growth hormones and antibiotics over any length of time.

Other dangerous toxins

Alcohol, Tobacco, Teflon, Heavy Metals, Illegal Drugs, Disinfectants, Synthetic Clothes and Fabrics, Vehicle exhaust, Cosmetics and Occupational chemical exposure.

IS PROCESSED FOOD GOOD FOR YOU?

Decreased nutrient value and unknown risks concerning packaging, transport, additives, preservatives, colourings, flavours, thickeners, sweeteners and so on are a problem because studies concerning long term consumption are incomplete and many of the chemicals are relatively recent. The countries that have food content regulators are finding that the fast- food production companies employ enormous numbers of scientists who are discovering more and more chemicals that preserve, improve flavour, colour, odour and generally make their products more appetising and addictive. The regulators can hardly keep up, possibly jeopardising consumer's health.

Additives of no nutritional value replace the nutrients naturally occurring in foods. It is difficult to avoid additives but they should be seen as toxic. Britain allows

15 colourings but Sweden and Norway permit none. There are worrying inconsistencies between nations.

As for processed food in general, you must draw your own conclusion. It contains much less nutritional value, minerals have been destroyed and it contains toxins and poses many unanswered questions regarding safety if consumed for many years. Increasingly, problems are being unearthed in research, which are never far from the news bulletins. On an almost daily basis we read, or see on TV, some sort of research which tells us that it is good to eat or drink something because it means we can live healthier, only to be confounded a week later by another report. It all depends upon who is funding the research and for what reason. It is not difficult to learn that the research details are announced by the beneficiaries of the results and usually correspond with increased profits and all this information may increase anxiety unduly and alter lifestyles accordingly but unnecessarily.

The messages are confusing. In general, people are getting fatter, but living longer. Obesity is costing a heap of money. Sickness is costing taxpayers a fortune via the health services. Poor, processed food diets can lead to obesity and sickness but people want to eat conveniently and cheaply without having to cook. This is daft because the food is not cheaper. One small bag of crisps is cheap but a crisp eater will eat more than one small bag in a day.

CRISP

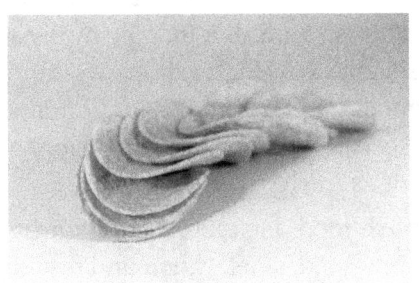

High in niacin but over 1,000 mg of salt per small packet. The calories are very high. Some research has suggested a link between cancer and crisps due to the altered chemical state of the cooking oil, which reaches colossal temperatures.

If the actual value of processed food is compared to the actual value of the unprocessed equivalent food, the processed food is more expensive because you need to eat 3 times as much of it to achieve the same nutritional value as the unprocessed equivalent. In addition, you are consuming all the required additives and preservatives which prevent processed food from perishing so rapidly and these almost always include salt and or sugar which all adds to the toxic load.

Grazing all day on empty fast foods is just not going to satisfy appetite but will add calories. Hunger is ever present. The obese are in fact malnourished.

Vast sums of money are invested in marketing and packaging and finding ways of persuading people to buy new foods but it is all for profit and not for health. Be very wary of all the hype associated with this industry and stick to the common sense of fresh food, lots of vegetables and fruit and almost no packaged foods at all. That way you will keep well.

I have no idea what proportion of supermarket space is dedicated to fresh foods but judging by my supermarket visits it is less and less. Increasingly we see 'fresh' foods flown in from all parts of the world. I often wonder how long the food exists from picking or packing to eating but I never regard it as fresh.

Unlike fresh food, processed food stores and travels well, often looks good, smells good and tastes good. It can be cheaper than non-processed food and packages easily. It often requires no preparation. It is convenient but by comparison with fresh food, is empty, has almost no fibre and requires a lot of energy to digest. I think of it as hollow food.

Processed foods diet: Healthy food diet

Taking 63 processed foods totalling 1.5 kilos and 49 healthy foods totalling 1.5 kilos you can see the remarkable difference in total values.

	Processed	Healthy
Protein	77	50
Fats	116	40
Carbohydrates	284	300
Fibre	18	60
Calories	2403	2200

Apart from the high fat and low fibre content, the average for vitamins and minerals in the processed diet is absolutely abysmal with the added disadvantage of a very poor sodium/potassium and calcium/magnesium ratio. The high levels of refined fats and sugars squeeze out the valuable nutrients from this diet. White flour is processed enabling the sugars to reach the blood very quickly which makes the body produce more insulin which takes the sugar into the body's cells and because so much insulin is produced, the sugar levels in the blood drop just as rapidly as they rose, leading to the body requiring another shot of sugar to sustain normal energy levels. We need carbohydrates for our energy but we need it constantly and not in short bursts. Processed foods give us short bursts of energy and this becomes habit forming, a little like drug dependency.

Sausages, pasties, fish cakes, fish fingers, grill steaks, luncheon meats, pork pies, sausage rolls, scotch eggs, steak and kidney pies.

Due to the requirement to keep these foods for as long as possible before throwing them away, the salt content is dreadfully high with an average of 1000 mg. for each portion of each food. There is also a very low amount of potassium (alkaline) averaging about 200 mg. for each portion of each food. Calcium is about 40 mg as against 15 mg for magnesium, which means that these foods are acid forming and give us high levels of fat and the wrong sort of quick release energy. One rasher of bacon gives us 8 gms of protein, 23 gms of fat and 240 calories. Salt comes in at 829 mg, and there are almost no vitamins or minerals. All the above are hopeless but tasty foods.

BACON RASHER

Protein	13
Fats	21
Carbohydrates	12
Fibre	0
Minerals	**
Vitamins	*
Calories	300

MARGARINE

Protein	0.1
Fats	38
Carbohydrates	0
Fibre	0
Minerals	*
Vitamins	*
Calories	351

The salt:potassium ratio is 158:1 in favour of salt, much higher than for butter. It is good for retinol and Vitamin D but has no minerals. This is no better than butter.

VEGETABLE OIL

Protein	0
Fats	25
Carbohydrates	0
Fibre	0
Minerals	**
Vitamins	*
Calories	224

No Vitamins and no minerals but we cook with it so do not think much of it. Problems arise when it is heated because heating changes it chemically.[43]

CANNED CHICKEN SOUP

Protein	6
Fats	10
Carbohydrates	20
Fibre	0
Minerals	**
Vitamins	*
Calories	200

Vegetable and chicken soup have good levels of folate. Tomato soup has 600 mcg of carotene, which is good. Salt is averaged at 1,900 milligms per can. Potassium is around 385 mg, magnesium is about 25 mg, iron is 2.1 and zinc is 1.2 but there are almost no vitamins at all.

CHIPS

Protein	15
Fats	30
Carbohydrates	140
Fibre	20
Minerals	**
Vitamins	**
Calories	800

Oven chips, instant mash, croquettes and waffles. A portion of chips will give us 800 calories! Salt is 1,200 mg, potassium at 2,400 mg, and there is a good level of magnesium but there is nothing else worthwhile about these potato derivatives.

SPREADS – CHOCOLATE NUT SPREAD, HONEY, JAM, MARMALADE

Protein	0.2
Fats	0.8
Carbohydrates	8
Fibre	0
Minerals	**
Vitamins	*
Calories	40

These figures are for one bread slice portion.

SAUCES – BROWN, KETCHUP, SALAD CREAM, MAYONNAISE

ONE TABLESPOON

Protein	0.3
Fats	3
Carbohydrates	4
Fibre	0
Minerals	**
Vitamins	*
Calories	30

71 mg of potassium and brown sauce will give us a little carotene but this does not redeem these foods.

The Traditional English Breakfast!

2 x rashers of bacon 1 x sausage

1 x portion of baked beans

1 x tomato

2 x fried eggs

2 x toast spread with butter

The following are average:

Recommended daily intake of salt is: 1000 mg – **English Fry-up: 4000 mg.**

Recommended daily intake of protein: 75 gms – **English Fry-up: 125 gms.**

Recommended daily intake of fibre: 150 gms – **English Fry-up: 12 gms.**

Recommended daily intake of oils: 75 gms – **English Fry-Up: 150 gms.**

Daily calorie allowance: 1800–2400.

English fry-up: 1800

Some people believe that because they have physically demanding jobs, they require excess calories and proteins. Up to a point, but the nutritional value of a meal like the English Fry-up has so little nutritional value it's laughable and must be regarded as no more than a naughty treat with side effects.

Just to put this into context, a person having two rashers of bacon and one sausage as part of a Fry-up is going to consume 900 calories of energy, 39 gms of protein, 63 gms of fat, nearly 3,000 milligms of salt, a little niacin and some B12, no fibre, 12 gms of carbohydrates and almost no minerals or other vitamins. That is only a part of this meal.

A portion of baked beans will add 20 gms of protein, 3 gms of fat and 55 gms of carbohydrates, almost no fibre and about 250 extra calories.

Then of course there is the toast or fried bread, tomatoes, black pudding and two fried eggs which will increase protein, fat, salt and calories to still higher levels but with almost no fibre and terribly low levels of valuable nutrients and minerals.

There will be in the region of 1,800 calories with added sauces, margarine or butter etc. Protein and fat levels will be well in excess of the recommended daily allowance of 75 gms with the fat levels of the two rashers of bacon and one sausage being 63 gms.

The low level of carbohydrates is worrying too, since we should be looking at 250 gms a day but this meal gives us about 60 gms of the fast release or instant sugar type.

There is no fibre to speak of and the vitamin and mineral values are alarmingly poor. Now add a mug of tea or coffee with two sugars and a cigarette!

Apart from being a tradition it is still one of the most delicious meals on the planet so, if you know just how dreadful this meal is in terms of food values and you are prepared to risk the consequences of eating it, may I suggest you reserve it for a very occasional indulgent treat. But absolutely not, as a regular daily meal. That can only lead to a very unhealthy outcome.

PROCESSED CONFECTIONARY FOODS

ABOUT 20 gms OF:

From left to right: Chocolate biscuits, Fruit Cake, Jaffa Cake, Swiss Roll, Sweets (on average: KitKat, Liquorice Allsorts, Mars Bar, Toffees, Twix, and Milk Chocolate)

Protein	1.2	4	0.6	1	2
Fats	6	10	2	2	9
Carbohydrates	14	42	13	11	25
Fibre	0.5	2	0	0	0
Calories	107	263	70	65	187

CAFFEINE AND FIZZY DRINKS

Nothing like a cup of tea for all manner of occasions or a cup of coffee to give us a bit of a lift and now that the coffee industry has invented a cornucopia of coffee drinks, we find ourselves drinking much more milk than before. Latte or cappuccino means masses of milk. I saw a 'coffee' when I visited Manila in the Philippines which had cream, ice cream and 1,800 calories!

Flavonoids in tea have benefits because they are antibacterial, anti-viral, anti- inflammatory and have vasodilatory actions, which make the blood capillaries open up. They also act as toxin scavengers.[44]

In spite of these benefits, which incidentally, can be gained from eating apples, grapes and onions, the main concern is in the negative effects of caffeine.

Caffeine is a stimulant and six cups daily is classed as addictive. It affects the adrenal glands by stimulating the production of adrenaline and corticoid steroids and when additional adrenaline and steroids are produced naturally, it is for emergencies to fight or escape a danger and is a life-saving device to be used only when absolutely necessary. Sadly, much of modern life creates sufficient anxiety for the steady production of adrenaline and steroids leading to the feeling of stress, tension and an inability to relax.

Caffeine offers short bursts of adrenal energy with the side effects of leaving the individual tired, irritable and tense until the next 'shot' of caffeine is consumed.

Since the adrenal glands are also responsible for reacting in the same way when blood sugar levels are low, it follows that the individual who consumes caffeine will have the same sensations as someone who has low blood sugar levels: headaches, fatigue, anxiety and irritability. High levels of caffeine consumption will lead to all of these feelings.

The increasing number of individuals who experience low blood sugar levels are suffering from a combination of poor mineral balance, high sugar intake, poor bowel conditions and damage from the side effects of medical drugs. These things cause energy levels to drop, stimulating a desire for caffeine and sugar or something sweet e.g. chocolates, which are high in caffeine anyway.

Meat, dairy foods and processed wheat and sugars are all suppressive foods and not only require a lot of energy to digest them but also make the absorption and utilisation of minerals more difficult.

Without the right balance of minerals, proper blood sugar control is unlikely.

Where a person requires caffeine to lead a normal life, they need the adrenal release which the caffeine affects. This can lead eventually to exhaustion of the adrenal glands and anyone who is dependent upon high and regular intakes of caffeine in tea, coffee, chocolate or fizzy drinks such as colas, and high energy drinks, should be regarded as suffering profound nutritional imbalance and is heading for ill health.

ALTERNATIVES

Herbal teas without milk and sugar.

Rooibos tea has no caffeine but very low tannin levels and tastes more like tea. It is a good antioxidant as well. It is good with lemon or cinnamon and a drop of honey.

COLAS, LEMONADE, DRINKING CHOCOLATE, HORLICKS, INSTANT COFFEE, ORANGE SQUASH

Protein	1
Fats	1
Carbohydrates	25
Fibre	0
Minerals	*
Vitamins	*
Calories	110

There are almost no vitamins and very low minerals but a lot of sugar.

I would just add a word of warning here regarding colas and fizzy drinks.

Not only do they contain huge amounts of sugar, one small can contains the equivalent of seven heaped teaspoons of sugar, but those that use aspartame or saccharine or sugar tasting chemicals are at risk because these are known to erode the density of bone and rot the teeth. Black teeth in young children are now a common sight in western countries.

These drinks are absolutely dreadful for health and they should be avoided.

SUMMARY

A very studious and scientific book entitled 'Human Nutrition and Dietetics' by Garrow, James and Ralph (2002) covers this subject from a distinctly scientific viewpoint. On the subject of processed food they conclude that ...'Heat processing affects the chemical structure of food components. The nutritional properties of proteins and fats are affected more than those of carbohydrates. Losses of vitamins can be considerable.'

'Food producers are under economic pressure to supply foods acceptable to the consumer. This can have adverse effects on the nutritional quality of the foods produced; on the other hand, greater consumer awareness of the links between diet and disease has created a demand for lower levels of fat, salt and sugar in foods.'

Do the vast majority of consumers know anything about the link between diet and disease? And if they do, why are they so incapable of reducing fat, salt and sugar from their diets?

Garrow et al again ... 'With increasing urbanisation, the modern food industry developed out of the need to transport food safely and to move much of the traditional processing and cooking of food from the domestic kitchen to the factory.'

Who is in control of your kitchen and your cooking?

I find this last but honest finding probably the most difficult to digest if you will pardon the pun.

In plain English, the modern food industry does not want you to do the cooking because they make much more money doing it for you.

'Regarding consumer protection the picture becomes quite hazy. Consumer protection laws were initially enacted to prevent the fraudulent adulteration of food ...'

Food labelling is also regulated but although 'harmonisation was first directed at compositional standards, it is now aimed at labelling' but, it appears that for this to be effective, a programme of public education is also needed.

We are protected by the Food and Agriculture Organisation, The World Health Organisation of the United Nations, The Food advisory Committee of the UK, the Committee on Medical Aspects of Food Policy (COMA), the Committee on Toxicity (COT), The Advertising Standards Agency and The Scientific Steering Committee and eight Scientific Committees concerning consumer health protection. And all they can come up with is a mish-mash of labelling ideas on a public who quite frankly are nothing if not confused and therefore tend not to read the labels.

And at every supermarket, service station, petrol station, coffee shop, post office, mini market and so on, the most prominent items on display are the alcohol and sugary beverages, sweets, chocolates, crisps, buns, cakes and all those tempting highly processed, empty and toxic foods that make us fat, unwell, highly energised and hooked!

And the labelling? Do you read the label on the back of a bar of chocolate? And does the slogan 'SMOKING KILLS' or hiding cigarettes in cupboards make any difference to a smoker?

And lastly to the final somewhat woolly quote from the eminent Garrow.

'Health Education is not enough to cause dietary change. This is best achieved when government policy in economic, organisational and social measures encourages the choice of a prudent diet.'

What does this mean and how does a government promote a prudent diet? Is it not more prudent to learn about food quality, the body's requirement for good food and the joy of cooking? This would lead to better health and could be much more fun if it worked but as we are about to see, it doesn't. Much sterner measures are required.

Garrow, James and Ralph wrote their book twenty years ago. The only visible change since then has been the rise and rise in the popularity of junk food and the diminishing quality of mainstream food. This is not just happening in the developed more prosperous world. It is gaining traction across the planet as you are about to find out. The effects of junk food consumption concern not only your health, but the health of the planet too; the environment, the manner in which livestock is treated, the health services around the world, the economies of countries, particularly poorer ones. And the scale of the problem is growing at an alarming rate.

Chapter 10

Food Production and Land Distribution

I want you to imagine a map of the world for a moment. If you take a piece of paper and a pen, place the paper as a landscape. The greatest length at the top and bottom.

1. Draw a nice big lozenge shape on the left-hand side. This represents CANADA, U.S.A., CENTRAL AMERICA and SOUTH AMERICA. Now write 27.5% in the centre of your lozenger.

2. Draw a flat lozenger at the top and bottom of your page. These represent the ARCTIC and ANTARCTICA. Now write 5% in each lozenger.

3. Now draw a long cigar-shaped lozenger from beneath the ARCTIC lozenger to the right-hand side of your page and insert 19%. This represents RUSSIA, EUROPE and the 'STANS', e.g. KAZAKHSTAN.

4. Draw a bauble/circle in the middle at the right-hand side of your page and insert 7%. This is CHINA.

5. Underneath CHINA, draw a slightly larger circle and add 8%. This represents AUSTRALIA, NEW ZEALAND, INDONESIA, MALAYSIA, THAILAND, PHILIPPINES AND MYANMAR.

6. In the middle of the page draw a lozenger above ANTARCTICA up to RUSSIA and another one over it beneath RUSSIA and almost touching CHINA. Combined, they make a shape a bit like AFRICA

but extending to include INDIA, PAKISTAN, AFGHANISTAN and THE MIDDLE EAST. Add 26.5%.

7. Finally, add a little blob at the top of your CHINA circle and write 1%. This represents MONGOLIA. Now add a little blob to the top of your AFRICA lozenger and write 1%. This represents LIBYA.

This rough diagram will help you understand the size of areas I am about to discuss.

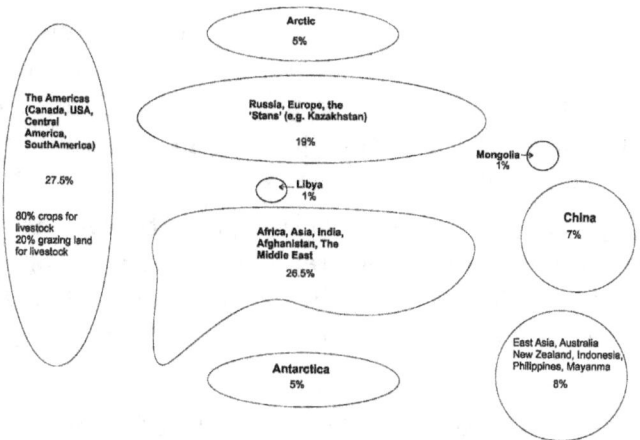

The land surface of our planet makes up 29% of the total. The remainder is Ocean (71%). 29% is also the amount of land surface unsuitable for human habitation, made up of glaciers, mountain ranges and deserts. An area the size of the ARCTIC, ANTARCTICA, RUSSIA and EUROPE. That leaves just 71% which is habitable, or 20.5% of the planet's total surface.

Nevertheless, most humans live in villages, towns or cities and if they were all squashed together, they would comprise an area the size of LIBYA. Yes, just 1% of the planet's land surface! The other small blob of just 1% -

MONGOLIA – represents all the rivers and inland lakes on the planet. Which leaves a lot of land.

The circle representing AUSTRALIA and the 'FAR EAST' – 8% – represents scrub. Not very fertile, not very accommodating. The big chunk in the middle of your page, AFRICA and INDIA and the MIDDLE EAST – 26.5% – represents the planet's forests. Most readers will know something about the value of forests and that chopping them down affects CO_2 levels in our atmosphere.

Now to the really important element of this exercise.

The smaller circle, CHINA, represents the amount of agricultural land dedicated to the growing of crops for human consumption. Grains such as wheat, rice and oats. Pulses and Legumes such as beans, lentils and chickpeas. Vegetables, Fruit, Nuts and Seeds.

The largest lozenger, which represents USA, Canada, Central and South America, represents the amount of land used for rearing and feeding livestock. Now write into this, the largest lozenger, 80% crops for livestock, 20% grazing land for livestock.

Let me do the calculation for you. We use 7% of the planet's land surface to grow crops for human consumption. Yet we use 22% of the planet's land surface to grow crops for animals which we subsequently eat. And a further 5.5% to graze them on. So animals or livestock, if you prefer, have the privilege and honour of access to 22% of the planet compared to the 7% humans utilise for the bulk of their food and adding just 1% for their homes!

O.K. This is not the precise picture, but it draws attention to the staggering imbalance of humanity's global food production.[45]

LAND USE BY FOOD TYPE

The efficiency of land used can be measured by the amount of land required to produce 100 gms of protein. In a chart produced by V. Poore and T. Nemecek (2018 for *Our World in Data.org*) we see that Sheep require 184.8m^2 to produce 100 gms of protein and Beef Cattle require 163.6m^2. 100 gms of cheese requires 39.8m^2 and Milk, 27m^2. Pigs need just 10.7m^2 and Chickens only 7.1m^2. It is crystal clear that consuming lamb and beef creates enormous demands on land use. Beef cattle and chickens are reared in enormous quantities by the fast-food industry.

These figures represent global averages. Individual countries will show differences to those shown as a global average.

Interestingly, since the industrial revolution, globally, the amount of land used for grazing cattle and sheep has quadrupled, implying that as wealth and prosperity increases, so does the consumption of meat. The amount of land used for agriculture globally has remained relatively static since 1960 which emphasises that more and more land is being used to rear livestock, but mainly cattle and sheep, and less land is being used for growing crops for human consumption. We must factor in too that the last 50 years have seen the global population double. Since agricultural land area has remained relatively static, we have to make two assumptions. Twice as many people are being fed from the same area of land as 50 years ago. However, four times as much land is being used for grazing sheep and cattle, emphasising the growing global demand for meat. This must, by any logical argument, put pressure on land availability for crops for human consumption.

All the data for future population growth estimates that by 2050 the world's population will reach about

10 billion, up from 7 billion. The reckoning is that the Americas and Europe and Russia will remain static but Asia to include China and India will increase by a quarter to 4 billion and Africa will double to 4 billion.

Individuals have their own ideas on what an emerging economy looks like, but clearly, the greatest demand for more meat will come from nations which have ambitions to become more advanced, more prosperous. And those nations include India, China and East Asia, but many African countries have ambitions too.

The obvious conclusion is that as peoples from relatively poor nations raise their personal wealth, they will almost certainly demand more meat. This, as you will read later, is exactly what the fast-food industry understands, putting even more pressure on land availability for crops for human consumption.

Chapter 10(A)
Food Production – Land Use

Of the crops, Cereals require the lion's share of the land, followed by Grains, Oil Crops or oil equivalents. Now, we know that crop growing for humans utilises just 7% of agricultural land, but crop growing for animals utilises 22%, and meadowland for grazing animals utilises 5.5%. So we have to deduce that most of the cereals, grains and oil crops are not for human consumption, but for animals, mainly cattle. Here in Devon, UK, where I live, a mainly agricultural county, the ratios are different. Of the agricultural land available, 54% is used for grazing, 20% for crops for animals and just 5% for crops for humans.[46] Many of our farmers, quite rightly, claim that their beef and mutton is more healthy due to the high percentage of grazing animals against those kept and fed indoors. But that doesn't alter the pathetically low percentage of land utilised for growing crops for humans.

LAND USE AND HEALTH

Having established that there is a remarkable difference between the land we use to rear livestock and the land we use to grow crops for humans, we must ask the question, WHY?

A lot of people believe it is important to provide adequate protein for the world's population. Others will add the importance of calories as a major requirement.

Government food regulators usually use calories and protein as a measure of food adequacy seemingly forgetting the importance of fibre, vitamins and minerals. So, we come to the acid test.

In a report by Hannah Richie for *Our World in Data* (2019), she found that the global supply of calories provided by plant-based foods is 82% and meat and dairy just 18%.

Similarly, global protein supply from plant-based foods is 63% and from meat and dairy just 37%. So we have this extraordinary situation where 77% of agricultural land provides 18% of total calories, and 37% of total protein, whilst just 23% of agricultural land provides 82% of calories and 63% of protein. So to all those people who are in favour of meat production and consumption, and use the argument that it is essential for the provision of protein and calories, I would say: "What utter nonsense!".

There is a correlation between wealth and meat consumption per annum. I will be dwelling on this in a later chapter, but it is significant at this point. These are my findings from the Food and Agriculture Organisation of the UN and compiled by the World Bank in 2020.

Average Income $ Per Annum		Average kg of beef
USA	65,000	125
Australia	50,000	120
European Union Average	45,000	80
Switzerland	65,000	65
China	17,000	65
India	6,000	3
Nigeria	5,000	4

Chapter 11

Food Production – Farming Methods

One of the most difficult questions regarding food production is "Are consumers driving food production methods or are the food producers creating the demand?" Farming methods are changing rapidly and many societies are finding it hard to keep up.

CAFOs

Concentrated Animal Feeding Operations (CAFOs)

CAFOs are indoor farms on a mass scale. Most poultry were raised in CAFOs in the 1950s and most cattle and pigs in the 1970s and 1980s. By the mid-2000s CAFOs dominated livestock and poultry production in USA and their market share is increasing. In 1966 it took 1 million farms to house 57 million pigs. By 2001, it took only 80,000 farms to house the same number.[47]

CAFOs are controlled by regulators, one of which is the Environment Protection Agency (EPA). They have created three categories – small, medium and large – according to the type of livestock. E.g. 1000 or more cattle constitutes a large CAFO, but 750 pigs, or less, constitute a small one. But size is all. The largest have up to 50,000 cattle and 500,000 chickens all indoors. A large CAFO must comply with regulations under the Clean Water Act (CWA) but small ones are subject on a case-by-case basis. A small CAFO can be recognised if it discharges pollutants into waterways via a road, ditch or pipe, but it can be certified as an Ordinary feeding operation (OFO) feeding operation (AFO) once its waste management system is certified on site.

Environmental Impact

Millions of tons of manure are produced. Treatment plans are in place, the most common being anaerobic lagoons which have contributed significantly to environmental health problems.

Water quality and aquatic ecosystems are often at serious risk of pollution from nitrogen and phosphorus, organic matter, spilled feed, bedding and litter material, hair, feathers, and animal corpses, Pathogenic bacteria and viruses, salts, arsenic, CO_2, methane, hydrogen sulphide, ammonia, antibiotics, pesticides and hormones. Now there's a tasty cocktail! The biggest 'spill' to date occurred in 1995 in N. Carolina when an 11,000m^2 lagoon burst. It released nearly 26 million gallons of effluent into the New River, killing 10 million fish and causing an outbreak of skin irritation and cognitive problems for those living in close proximity of the spill.[48]

Air Quality

CAFOs produce ambient air quality – ammonia, hydrogen sulphide, methane and particulate matter. They also emit strains of antibiotic resistant bacteria. Livestock waste is sprayed onto nearby fields and some is carried in the air to nearby populations. Eye irritants, ammonia and hydrogen sulphide are included.

Economic Impact

In USA in the 1930s there were approximately 7 million farms. Now there are fewer than 2 million. However, 98% of them are family owned, but most meat and dairy products are produced in CAFOs. They provide low-cost animal products: meat, milk and eggs. They are efficient and can produce animal products cheaply, which, of course, has increased their popularity and demand. According to Christopher Delgado, "milk production has doubled, meat has tripled, and eggs quadrupled since 1960 in USA."[49] This is good news for the consumer and for the handful of CAFO operators and their backers. But not for the 98% of small farmers!

Negative Impact

- Damaging effects to the environment.
- Damaging effect upon local populations and their health.
- Contract farming enables corporations to avoid waste management issues and costs.
- Property values near CAFOs plummet.
- CAFOs benefit from tax breaks and subsidies.
- Anti- competitive practices create monopolies.
- Overuse of antibiotics.

- Low income and minority populations suffer disproportionally, created by low-cost housing and access to low wage employment.

Animal Welfare Concerns

There are a number of reports which raise concerns regarding animal welfare at CAFOs. Not surprisingly. According to David Nibert of Wittenberg University, more than 10 billion animals are housed in doubtful conditions in more than 20,000 CAFOs in USA alone. It is not hard to imagine the conditions of confinement and the need for antibiotics to prevent disease. The fact that these animals are fed, not with grass – their natural food – but with maize, soya, wheat and canola generates massive demand for land. Most of the Brazilian forest clearance is for animal food.

CAFOs are not the preserve of USA. They are found all over the world. The production of chicken meat in Thailand follows the same system pattern as beef production in USA. China and Brazil produce nearly 30 million metric tons of chicken meat annually, with much of it packaged for export.

Regulation of CAFOs is haphazard. Governments and States use differing yardsticks and therefore the levels of humane treatment of animals are often dubious, as is the health of the end product. The impact upon the environment and on local communities varies too according to regulations and controls. The impact upon human health and upon global warming will be covered in later chapters, but for now, let us be clear.

CAFOs, large and small, dominate the farming of livestock worldwide. A few dominant corporations control these food 'factories'. Their aim is to dominate the production of livestock worldwide. Due to scale, they are able to produce meat and dairy produce at low cost to the consumer. But much is compromised. The nutrient quality of the end product. The health of the end product. The quality of life for the animals, and for those employed in the industry. The impact upon the local environment and those living in close proximity to the plant. The impact upon small scale farmers. The impact upon global warming. The impact upon the health of the consumer. And finally. By producing meat products so cheaply, it is damaging the demand for plant-based foods which are, collectively, better for human health. When this effect reaches populations in developing countries, the impact is catastrophic, as we shall see.

Chapter 12

Food Waste

About one-third of the world's food is thrown away.[50] The United Nations Environment Programme analysis estimated that global food waste was 931 million tonnes equating to the equivalent of 121 kilos per person living on the planet. 61% from households, 26% from food services and 13% from retailers.[51] Bearing in mind that millions of people worldwide are close to starving, this information does not rest well on the more prosperous.

Furthermore, due to food waste, 2.2 billion tons of CO_2 are emitted annually.[52] It doesn't take a genius to work out the damage caused through land use, water use and the loss of biodiversity. Economically, it is beyond foolish, since roughly a third of all land and water utilised in global food production could be saved to better purposes and the loss of biodiversity reduced by a third. This is so serious that in 2022 at the United Nations Biodiversity Conference, nations agreed to reduce food waste by 50% by 2030. The question is whether the 'nations' have either the appetite or the teeth to implement their aim. I am doubtful.

Just to be clear, food redirected to animal feed, composted or used as bioenergy does not count as waste, but instead, qualifies as unavoidable food waste! I was under the impression that waste, by its very nature, is avoidable!

In the USA food which is recovered and donated to feed people (food banks) is known as 'excess food'. 'Food Loss' is unused product such as unharvested crops, and 'Food Waste' is food which is served but not eaten, spoiled food, peels and rind considered inedible and sent for animal consumption, composted, anaerobically digested, sent to landfill or used to produce energy.

There are many differing interpretations of 'Food Waste' but none are able to mitigate the overall tragedy of waste. It is hard to imagine, but some food waste is deliberate. In 2013 the Natural Resources Defence Council of the USA suggested that the leading cause of food waste in America is due to uncertainty over food expiration dates – 'best-before', 'sell- by' or 'use-by' dates.[53] Consumers are uncertain and cautious enough to jettison food because they think it may be unsafe. Retailers too throw away large quantities of food motivated by the expiration dates. They also contribute to waste due to their contractual arrangements with suppliers. Failure to supply agreed quantities renders farmers or processors liable to cancellation, consequently producing more than required to increase the margin for error. Surplus produce is dumped.

Retailers also have cosmetic standards for produce. Misshapen vegetables, bruised fruit, never reach the shelves. In the USA, about 3 million tonnes (3 billion kg) of produce is wasted each year because of appearance.[54] I have to stop for a moment, take a deep breath, and ask myself: 'What sort of a society creates people who throw away a perfectly good tomato, potato or onion because it is not perfectly formed?' In Europe 40%–60% of fish caught are discarded as the wrong size or the wrong species, creating 2.3 million tons per annum in the North Atlantic and North Sea. Wasted. Is this not shocking?[55]

Most of the food wasted in developed countries is produced post-consumer, driven by low prices, greater disposable income, consumer expectations of food-cosmetic standards and an increasing lack of production knowledge.[56]

An American friend complained to a restaurant owner friend of his, that the portions were too big. He was unable to consume the amount of pasta on his plate and would prefer to eat half the amount and pay half the price. The restaurant owner replied that he made a nice profit on his gargantuan $18 serving, and that a $9 serving would only cover the costs of his overheads. The difference in the cost of a $9 and $18 serving was minute, so he was not perturbed by the waste.

Once again, we witness the association between the relatively prosperous who can afford to waste food and the less well-off.

In the developing countries, estimates of between 400–500 calories per day per person are wasted. In industrialised countries, the estimate is 1,500 calories per person per day. In the former, 40% of waste occurs at post-harvest and processing stages, but in the latter 40% waste occurs at retail and consumer stages, and this amounts to 222 million tonnes, which is equivalent to the entire food production in sub-Saharan Africa.[57] On average, 20 kg p.a. of food is wasted per individual per annum. In the industrialised countries, that figure is 90 kg. It seems the more prosperous we become, the more we waste. In Canada, for example, 58% of all food is wasted.[58] In the U.S.A., according to a 2004 report from the University of Arizona, 14%–15% of edible food is untouched or unopened, amounting to $43 billion worth of discarded but edible food. Is there an excuse for this?

There are many reasons for food waste, but perhaps the most perverse is the disturbing fact that for the biggest multinational food manufacturers and retailers, food waste increases profit. The more food produced, shipped, processed, and sold, the greater the profit. It doesn't matter if it's discarded. It's done its job. It's increased profit. For consumers discarding food is not profitable, and amounts to a waste of money. So why do people waste it? I can only assume that those who discard their food, whether it's into the pedal bin or left on a plate in a diner, have sufficient funds not to care.

I return to the beginning of this chapter. The global food production industry accounts for over 25% of total greenhouse gas emissions creating global warming. One-third of the food produced is wasted, accounting for 8% of total greenhouse gas emissions. Is it not logical and sensible for those of us who inhabit a developed country to make a concerted effort to reduce global warming by NOT discarding food, and at the same time, save money?

Chapter 13

Food Production and Health

Industrialised food production delivers low cost, low nutrient food in excessive quantities. The dichotomy facing governments around the world is choosing between cheap, empty yet abundant food which becomes available to even the poorest members of society, or increasing regulation which would inevitably increase costs and possibly quality. However, there is another element yet to be factored into the equation. What is the cost of treating a sick society, and shouldn't this be taken into consideration by government food regulators?

Let's return to the production of cheap food. The negative elements have already been discussed.

1. The use of chemicals to generate higher yields – fertilisers.
2. The run off effect of fertilisers into rivers and upon microbes in the soil.
3. The use of pesticides and herbicides which can transmit into the food chain.
4. The treatment of livestock, particularly in CAFOs.
5. The use of antibiotics to prevent disease in high density farming practices.
6. The effects upon the labourers and local residents around CAFOs.
7. The storage of highly toxic waste.
8. The interference of genetic modification and engineering techniques in plant food.

9. The deforestation of valuable CO_2 sinks being replaced by crops for the specific consumption by livestock kept indoors.

10. The control of global food production by fewer and fewer players.
11. The increase in preservative chemicals in addition to salt and sugar.
12. The increase in packaging to safeguard product in transit and extend shelf life.
13. The increase in advertising as processed food outlets increase global reach.
14. The very real problems, now being discovered, created by the use of antibiotics in mass food production.

There are many other negative elements in the production of processed food, but I want to draw attention in particular to the last element.

ANTIBIOTICS IN FOOD PRODUCTION

Imagine if you can, a CAFO of 50,000 cattle and 500,000 chickens, all indoors and fed mainly on soya, maize, wheat and canola (rape seed). The very close crowding of livestock can easily lead to disease, so antibiotics are used to prevent this. Although regulators are concerned that the overuse of antibiotics can lead to resistance, it is almost impossible to prevent their use in conditions found in industrialised livestock farming.[59]

Naturally enough, the use of antibiotics continues in the effort to produce cheap food.

There is, however, relatively new and perhaps even more pernicious evidence of another side effect of antibiotic use in industrialised mass livestock rearing. Marty Blaser[60] was concerned at the growth in obesity in the U.S.A., where over 34% of adults are obese. The correlation between the presence of antibiotics from the food chain and the rise in levels of obesity is disturbing. Blaser became so concerned that he ran tests on mice. He took some young laboratory mice and created two groups. Group A were fed antibiotics causing them to grow more rapidly, with an increase in weight and body fat. Those in the group which were also fed a high-fat diet grew even bigger. Group B were fed a normal diet.

Returning to the livestock in CAFOs or industrialised farming units which is where most fast-food meat is reared, cattle reach slaughter age at 14 months, weighing in at around 550 kg. They eat mass produced maize, soya, wheat – feed laced with low-dose antibiotics – supposedly to resist diseases. Regulators have become concerned about the use of antibiotics in farming but have to accept their use in preventing illness. Whether it's cattle for burgers, chickens for nuggets or fish for fingers, you can be certain that antibiotics have been used and consequently you may be vulnerable.

Marty Blaser continued his experiments on mice and found that, apart from increases in weight and body fat, once the antibiotic use ceased, and returning to a normal diet, the group A mice remained fat. In addition, their immune systems had been compromised creating less protection from disease. Blaser hadn't finished. He planted gut scraping from antibiotic fed mice (group A) into the gut of antibiotic-free mice (group B) which continued to be fed on a normal antibiotic-free diet. These healthy mice made evident weight gains. The problem lay in alterations to elements of the digestive system that reduces food transit time which reduces the time available for the absorption of nutrients, but with an increase in the extraction of calories. The effect is almost permanent hunger and greater capacity to absorb calories.

O.K., so these experiments were carried out on mice. But surely there must be something similar occurring in human populations. And consider this. Since antibiotic use in food production is so rife, and the evidence of the presence of antibiotic particles in our water and our food chain, including milk, isn't it highly likely that new-born babies are at greater risk from the effects of antibiotic presence in their mothers? Are not young children caught up in an obesity epidemic through no fault of their own?

The research is not definitive, but I believe that the use of antibiotics in food production and in farming is causing untold harm and creates, over time, some of the most urgent issues regarding people's health.

OBESITY

Is obesity a disease? Is it O.K. to be overweight because it isn't obesity? As we are beginning to see, increasing numbers of very young children are born to be overweight through no fault of their own. But, as almost everyone knows, the majority of people who are overweight are almost guaranteed to suffer from chronic health conditions sooner than those who are not overweight. We almost certainly know what sort of diseases are chronic too. Heart failure, stroke, respiratory problems, digestive issues, allergies, joint deterioration, and most obvious of all, eternal fatigue. And we have seen the outcomes of endless fatigue as we explained in earlier chapters. And what of the mental issues associated with being overweight?

The World Obesity Federation (www.worldobesity.org) has compiled some of the most recent statistics (2022) from which I have extrapolated the following data.

1. On current trends obesity will cost the global economy over $4 trillion of potential income in 2035 which is 3% of current global domestic product (GDP).
2. Countries' current health system responses to Obesity and non-communicable diseases (NCDs) such as heart failure and cancer have been recorded.

In Low Income Countries:		
With Obesity (millions)	2025	2035
Boys	5	11
Girls	6	13
Men	12	26
Women	31	64
Economic Impact (billions in $)	5	9
Middle Income:		
Boys	70	87
Girls	42	62
Men	167	268
Women	208	291
Economic Impact $billion	699	1,660
High Income	2025	2035
Boys	24	29

Girls	16	20
Men	160	211
Women	153	191
Economic Impact $billion	1,610	2,270

Obesity, like population growth, is increasing massively over 10 years and the economic costs also doubling. Unless economies in low-income countries also double, their populations will suffer from health services unable to cope with the growth in NCD's which will undoubtedly add untold pressure for greater migration. Add this pressure to the current pressures caused by global warming and you are facing catastrophe.

Low-income countries

Low-income countries, quite obviously, are the least prepared to cope with rising obesity levels and the diseases that arise from it.

Middle-income countries

Middle-income countries are seeing rises of about a third in obesity levels over the ten-year period from 2025–2035 but obesity levels are already higher than in low-income countries. This is not surprising because these countries have already experienced greater economic growth, and since increases in wealth correlate to increases in obesity, the pressures on health services increase accordingly.

High-Income Countries

2025 levels of obesity are lower than middle income populations and growth is only about 25% but economic impact doubles reflecting the high existing costs on a sector which will experience almost no population growth.

Perhaps the most astonishing comparisons concern the impact that obesity and its secondary diseases have upon economies. $5 billion in 2025 rising to $9b in 2035 in the world's poorest countries where populations are due to double. Against $1.6 trillion rising to $2.2 trillion in the world's wealthiest countries where populations are due to remain static. The global impact could be dramatic. Imagine, if you will, a member of a poor family of 10 children, all with access to cheap fast food, all trending towards obesity and its inherent diseases, e.g. diabetes.

Faced with an almost non-existent and distant health service, an increase in local food costs due to drought or flooding, difficulty finding work, poor education and a bleak future, the temptation to send one or more members of the family abroad to seek employment and enough funds to send financial aid back to the family is enormous. Migration is inevitable.

And this in turn will increase the pressure on health services in the countries which receive migrants.

These are just a few of the problems created by an increasingly powerful global food production system being embraced in all countries which reach a GDP commensurate with their profitability of the industry.

The Office for National Statistics (ONS) for the UK recently produced some stark statistics (July 2023).

More than 2.5 million people are 'economically inactive' because of long-term sickness of which almost 1 million had at least five health problems, says Jon Boys, senior labour market economist for the Chartered Institute of Personnel and Development. He says "It is becoming starker and starker that the UK population is sicker, and this is a problem." This is an understatement. The increase in multiple health conditions was particularly marked amongst younger workers. Of the 16- to 34-year-olds who were inactive in 2019 owing to long-term sickness, 17% had five or more health conditions. By 2023, this had risen to 23%. The trend is alarming. Jon Boys again: "It has a macro effect on the labour supply which is particularly acute in the UK at the moment."

Tina McKenzie, Federation of Small Businesses (FSB) policy chairman says: "Staff shortages are especially acute with the right skills as a problem for growth plans."

And, of course, it is not just in the UK that mass sickness is increasing, affecting economic growth; it is creeping right across the industrialised world and it will seep into emerging nations causing even greater problems.

Poor food, poor diets, as exemplified in the fast-food industry, and indeed, in the not so fast-food industry, is a major cause of long-term or 'chronic' sickness adding increasing pressure on health services and undermining economic growth.

And there is another issue. Being sick is no fun. As sickness levels rise, so too do misery levels and depression, not just amongst the elderly, but increasingly amongst the young. So much misery for so many young people. This really is not acceptable.

Chapter 14

Modified Food

Imagine if you will that you are a food producer. Someone comes along and suggests that production costs could be lowered by cramming livestock indoors under a controlled feeding system that achieves greater output in less time, thereby reducing costs and increasing profits. If the system received the go-ahead from the regulators, you'd jump at the opportunity. And so CAFOs (Concentrated Animal Feeding Operations) became the new production line for livestock. Since the system has the approval of regulators, the problems surrounding CAFOs are no longer your problems. Mankind is nothing if not inventive, always seeking ways to improve human existence.

In 4000 BC dairy farming began in Iraq, and Egyptians began using yeast to bake bread and make wine.

In 2000 BC Egyptians, Sumerians and the Chinese began making cheese.

In 1500 AD beneficial bacteria was being used to flavour and preserve foods such as sauerkraut and yoghurt.

In 1861 Louis Pasteur develops pasteurisation to preserve food by destroying microbes by heating. This is significant. We are now discovering that preserving food has benefits which sit alongside detriments.

In 1982 human insulin is genetically engineered.

In 1953 the double helix of DNA is explained.

In 1986 genetically engineered tobacco is grown.

In 1993 The US Food and Drugs Administration (FDA) approves a genetically engineered system to increase milk production, and Calgene Inc. market the first genetically engineered whole food in the U.S. food supply. A tomato.

1996 saw the first herbicide-tolerant soy bean in the U.S. Things are now beginning to take off in the GM world.

In 2006 GM rice is approved in the U.S.

In 2007 11 new pharmaceutical and industrial GM crops are approved.

The GM business is still in its infancy and debate rages around its benefits. Supporters claim that it can produce better taste, nutrition and quality. It increases profit for growers. It can produce crops which are virus and insect resistant and have a high tolerance to herbicides. It also increases food yield and therefore supposedly reduces world hunger. It is almost too good to be true!

However, there are problems. Many GM crops cannot re-seed. A subsistence farmer has to purchase new seed each year, which, of course, benefits the seed supplier. Being able to spray fields with herbicide (weed killer) without damaging crops is fine except that the chemical (usually Roundup) runs off and eventually settles as a residual in local waterways, affecting fish stocks.

Pesticides will destroy some pests enabling others to flourish but the wildlife that relied upon the destroyed pests have their food chain diminished which can interfere with natural food chains from tiny insects up to larger birds and animals. Increased food yields can lead to cheaper food but not necessarily in the areas where it is required, and where it exists in areas where it is <u>not</u> required, there is an increase in food waste.

Better taste, nutrition and quality is debatable. Anyone who is familiar with buying food and cooking it in the U.S.A. will testify to the gigantic size of fruits and vegetables, to their cosmetically attractive shapes and colours and to their tastelessness. The areas set aside in most U.S. supermarkets for organic fruit and vegetables is pitifully laughable.

Additionally, animal studies have identified risks with GM consumption –

Infertility

Immune system compromise

Accelerated aging

Altered genes associated with cholesterol synthesis, insulin regulation, cell signalling and protein formation.

Alterations in liver, kidney, spleen and gut function.

Four principles were established in 1986, in respect of GM of agricultural produce.

1. Existing laws are sufficient for regulation.
2. Regulation applies to products, <u>not</u> processes by which they were developed.
3. Safety to be assessed on a case-by-case basis.
4. Agencies should coordinate regulatory efforts. This new framework applies to drugs and foods.

All this requires collaboration between the United States Department of Agriculture (USDA), the Environmental Protection Agency (EPA) and the Food and Drug Administration (FDA). In other words, change has been almost outlawed thanks to the power of a vast bureaucracy.[61]

The Monsanto Company produced 'Roundup', a glyphosate-based herbicide, in the 1970s. It became the major producer of genetically engineered crops and began to apply biotechnology to agriculture using techniques developed by biotech drug companies.[62] Monsanto's roles in agricultural changes, biotechnology products, lobbying of government agencies and its roots as a chemical company have resulted in controversies. It manufactured 'insecticide DDT', 'PCBs' (chemicals found in paints, glue and plastics), Agent Orange (used in the Vietnam war as herbicides warfare) and recombinant bovine growth hormone.[63] Its seed patenting model was criticised as biopiracy[64] and a threat to biodiversity as invasive species.

The German chemical giant Bayer paid $66 billion in cash for Monsanto in 2018, and made further payments to settle lawsuits involving ex-Monsanto products – Roundup, PCBs and Dicamba.[65] None of this fosters confidence in the development and use of GM techniques by a chemicals behemoth.

The more I study the development of farming, food production, food wholesalers and retailers, the clearer the picture becomes. The U.S.A. is the leading nation and the powerhouse in these sectors so it is with fascination that I have observed the trends that are seeping into other continents on our planet.

As mentioned earlier, farming has moved from small, often family run units providing local produce for local populations with a minimum of exporting. Today, over

70% of farmed produce comes from industrialised farms producing cheap products on a gigantic scale specifically for export throughout a country, offering far less variety, cosmetically packaged, genetically altered, for transport and storage, often tasteless, nutritionally suspect, and universal. It is the sameness that is so disappointing. The marketing and packaging is stupendous, but, like Disneyland, the 'wow' factor soon wears off. I call it 'Disney food'. It tempts you with its packaging, colour, size and low cost, but its substance, the most important element, is distinctly disappointing. And furthermore, the savoury foods are, in my opinion, too salty. I don't cook with or add salt. And the sweet foods are too sweet. I don't have a sweet tooth. So why has the U.S. become so enamoured with mass food production?

Simple. It has no choice. The mass food industry is destroying small farms – they can't compete. The producers serve the supermarket chains, and the choice of chains is diminishing, like the farms. The bigger the chain, the greater the buying power. Think Asda, Lidl, Aldi and of the fast food chains: McDonalds, KFC and Dominoes.

And the greater the buying power, the greater the control. In Florida, I have watched the growth of one particular supermarket chain, 'Publix', at the expense of almost all others, diminishing choice to that of the management. It's a gradual move towards monopoly. And what is driving this activity? Power? Control? Profit? Perhaps all three. Whatever the answer, the produce, whilst attractive to the eye, is bland at best and in some cases, perhaps, suspect.

It is sad to record that in general our food seems to be less tasty. Perhaps it's my taste buds giving up as I get older. Even in food famous France, there are disappointments. The days spent observing French shoppers picking up Cantaloupe melons, sniffing and squeezing before making their choice at fruit and vegetables stalls in outdoor markets seem to have disappeared., Why? Because the melons are probably genetically altered. Ripening of Cantaloup melons occurs rapidly as the fruit produces an enzyme which enables it to 'explode' its ripening process and softening and producing a smell which shoppers tested by sniffing and squeezing! But the rapid ripening created up to 30% of waste as melons ripened before purchase, which in turn hindered transport further.

So along come the scientists, snipping and slicing until they produced a 'synthetic promoter' which reduces the 'ethylene synthesis' – ripening.[66] Now, melons are bland, tasteless and hard but available, and the waste is simply transferred from the supermarket and market stall waste bin, to the household waste bin. Who wants to eat a hard, tasteless melon?

The food industry is doing everything it can to get produce to market, regardless of distance.

The produce is recreated to look attractive and is cosmetically engineered to appeal to an increasingly fussy market accustomed to a Disneyesque, botoxed, fantasy world of perfection. We're talking about fruit and vegetables here. Not a star of stage and screen, although the stars of food are burgers and pizzas. But it seems that thanks to the colossal budgets and imaginative designers, the advertising and marketing of food focuses more on appearance than on content. How else does fast food increase in popularity?

An education officer from a slowly drowning Pacific Island, concerned that obesity in children was reaching unacceptably high levels, remarked that in spite of their schools offering courses in cooking and nutrition, the first thing the pupils did at the end of the school day was to visit the nearest fast food takeaway. The marketing, packaging, price, allure as a cool venue for kids, the taste and smell all create the right atmosphere for youngsters who become addicted, yes, truly, addicted to fast food. These places are seen as birthday party venues and places to go for a treat.

Chapter 15

Fast Food – the American Story

The Appetiser

1. Most Americans eat fast food 1–3 times a week.
2. One third of Americans are eating fast food on any given day.
3. Ages 20–39 eat the most fast food (44.9%).
4. Men eat more than women.
5. 83% of Americans eat at fast food restaurants at least once a week.
6. 10% of annual income is spent on fast food.
7. Those earning more money eat more fast food.
8. More fast food is eaten at lunchtime.
9. 34% of children eat fast food daily.
10. Fast food increases the risk of obesity, heart disease, depression and type 2 diabetes.
11. Regular fast food consumption increases 2.2% annually.
12. McDonald's is the most popular restaurant with $130.4 billion being spent in their outlets worldwide.

The Main Course

Almost 45% of 30–40-year-olds eat fast food on any given day whereas only 24% of 60+ year-olds do. Why? Do the elderly cook? Do they prefer fresh food? Do they have enough money?

African Americans consume 42%, White Americans 38%, Hispanic 35% and Asian 30%. However, the average American adult (whoever that is!?) spends $1,200 annually on fast food alone, which nationally in total could (and this is staggering) which could end world hunger for up to 3 years.[67]

Why is Fast Food So Popular?

1. It saves time. No preparation, no shopping, no cooking, sometimes no exiting the home – just pick up the phone and order it in. 20% of fast food is eaten in the car! Yum yum!
2. It's cheap. Well, er, it's cheaper than other restaurants, but it's cheaper still to cook at home. 32% of people in America eat fast food because they think it's cheaper than cooking at home.

Personally I find it extraordinary that many American homes have enormous kitchens, huge cookers and cavernous fridge-freezers, massive microwave ovens and drawers full of utensils, all seldom used. The barbeque and the microwave oven may be used more frequently, and the fridge-freezer is often full of foods that may only see the waste bin, but even with all that kitchen luxury, imported Uber eats pizzas and burgers take precedence!

The lower the income, the less fast food. Isn't that peculiar? Why would more wealthy people prefer to eat junk food rather than a half decent restaurant meal or a meal at home? Perhaps it's the lure of fast food. The smell, the taste, the colour, the temptation.

Or maybe, it's just more convenient.

There are 826,000 fast food restaurants worldwide and rising. There's always one close by, wherever you are in the world. It tastes good too. High in calories, loaded with fat and sugar and salt, our taste buds love it. Most nutrition that should be present, has been stripped away due to processing, so those things – fat, salt and sugar – are added to make the food taste good. Combine that with a caffeine or sugar-laden soft drink (soda) and it's no wonder we hit that workday slump at around 3.00 pm. Fast food might taste and smell good, and it may look good, but it really has very little in the way of good substance. Nutritionally, it's poor, hence the name 'junk food'.

Not only are there close to a million outlets worldwide, but the industry employs 13 million people, so it's safe to say, it's here to stay.

There are, on average, 836 calories in a fast-food meal. Consumption of fast food at least twice a week can double your risk of type 2 diabetes and even just living near a fast food restaurant is linked to a 5.2% greater risk of obesity. (Schools beware) it's the temptation! The risk of depression is increased by 51% in regular fast-food consumers. The problem, simplified, is that in order to manufacture food that can be cooked quickly and be relatively shelf stable, the process strips the food of its vital nutrients and fibre, replacing them with salt and sugar and fats. It's no wonder we don't feel great when we eat a lot of fast food.

All the above statistics have been provided by the Barbecue Lab in 2023 (www.thebarbecuelab.com).

The internet abounds with information and therefore advice regarding the dangers of consuming too much fast food. Governments the world over are seeking ways of reducing its popularity. Doctors are fighting a losing battle fixing people suffering from obesity-related illnesses. Health services are desperate for more funds to help treat obesity-related diseases. Mental health specialists and now A and E departments, are seeing increasing numbers of depressed patients.

And now we see the advent of weight loss injections with regulations in tatters in UK. Mountjaro, Wegovy and Saxenda seem to be the leaders and tempting offers are being deployed to persuade millions to part with their money.

These products may lead to weight loss but don't change the diet. Instead of millions of overweight sick people heading for the hospitals there will be queues of slimmer sick (and maybe poorer) people lining up at the hospital gates.

Farmers are leaving their farms in droves, unable to make a living and handing over their land to the corporations now dictating farming and controlling output. As countries emerge from poverty, so the fast-food industry enters, taking up its position on the high streets. Glamourous frontages, bright lights, colourful interiors, cheap, colourful, tasty fast food and sodas, irresistible and filling – for a short while. You really can't blame people, especially youngsters, for inhabiting these places habitually. How often have you said, or heard, "and if you're really good, we'll go for a pizza?" Yes, something as bland and unexciting as a pizza is considered a 'treat'. And how many of you have taken a child to a 'McDonalds' for a birthday party? Is it any wonder more and more people regard fast food as a way of life.

Chapter 16

Food Production and Climate Change

Food needs to be grown, processed, transported, distributed, prepared, consumed and sometimes thrown away. Each step creates greenhouse gas emissions (GGEs). About one third of the world's total emissions is caused by food production, from field to fork. Most of it stems from agriculture and land use, and includes:

Methane from cattle's digestive system.

Nitrous Oxide from fertilisers used to increase crop yield.

Carbon Dioxide from destroying forests to create more land for grazing and crops.

Emissions from manure, animal waste and food waste, rice cultivations, burning of crop residues and fuel used in agriculture and food processing.

To a lesser extent, but nevertheless, significant:

Refrigeration and transport of foodstuffs.

Industrial processes, e.g. packaging.

Food waste. 8% of global GGEs.

Animal based foods, especially beef, dairy, farmed fish and seafood cause the most emissions because:

Meat production requires the most pasture which is often created by deforestation.

Cows and sheep emit methane which is much more 'potent' than CO_2, and beef is used increasingly in the rapid growth in fast food outlets.

Cattle waste on pastures and in CAFOs and chemical fertilisers used on crops such as maize, rape seed, soy and wheat for cattle feed, emit nitrous oxide which is even more 'potent' than methane.

Fish farms and especially 'shrimp' farms which occupy coastal areas once covered by mangrove forests which absorbed huge amounts of carbon. This carbon is released when the mangroves are destroyed to make way for shrimp farms.

PLANT-BASED FOODS

Fruit and vegetables, grains, beans, peas, nuts, lentils and spices use less land, energy, water and producing them creates extremely low levels of GGEs compared to meat and fish farming.

Kgs of GGEs produced for every kg	
Beef	Over 70 kg
Lamb	Over 40 kg
Cheese	24 kg
Breads and Pasta	1.6 kg
Vegetables	0.7 kg
Fruit	0.9 kg

Kgs of GGEs produced for every 100 gms of Protein	
Beef	35.6 kg
Lamb	20 kg
Cheese	11 kg
Breads and Pasta	1.3 kg
Vegetables	7 kg
Fruit	10 kg

Kgs of GGEs produced for every 1000 calories	
Beef	26 kg

Lamb	12
Cheese	6
Breads and Pasta	0.6
Vegetables	3
Fruit	1.5

From these figures it is irrefutable that meat production is by far the greatest emitter of GGEs. Fast food is frequently based around the production of meat; mainly beef and chicken. But also, and with less damage to the environment, the production of wheat for pastas and pizzas.[68]

When we pause for a moment to consider the consumption of meat, we have to conclude that we simply cannot continue to justify our continued consumption of it on the present scale.

It utilises 80% of all agricultural land. We grow crops for animal consumption on 48% of it while growing crops for us humans on only 20%. This is idiotic. Add to this the fact that the crops on our 20% provide us with 83% of our calories and 63% of our protein, while the remaining 80% provides only 17% of our calories and 37% of our protein.

Now we discover that meat production also produces by far the most greenhouse gases from all food production. It is not a particularly healthy food, nor particularly nourishing. Nevertheless, it is massively popular and the fast-food manufacturers and retailers have created an irresistible image for it.

Beyond meat, in the USA, 71% of all food is highly processed. Why? Because it is cheap to produce, can last for ages before rotting and be transported across continents – all very efficient and profitable. But is it good for you? And just as pertinent, is it good for the planet?[69]

HOW CAN FOOD-RELATED EMISSIONS BE REDUCED?

This requires changes at all stages, from field to fork, from farm to consumer.

1. Shift food systems away from meat production to plant production and plant-rich diets.
2. Utilise more plant protein from beans, chickpeas, lentils, nuts and grains.
3. Reduce animal-based foods (meat and dairy) and less saturated fats (butter, milk, cheese, meat, coconut and palm oil).

Animal production will always remain an important element of food consumption. It is important for food security, nutrition, and livelihoods for large numbers of rural populations around the world. But do we really need to eat so much of it?

Improved feeds and feeding techniques can reduce methane emissions – in addition to gases released from manure. Smaller herds, fewer and more productive animals can help. Much can be done to improve better agricultural practices and more intense regulation is required. And then of course, there's food waste. If food waste was a country, it would be the third-largest emitting country in the world after China and the U.S.A.[70]

It doesn't cost us anything to waste less food. In fact, we can save money. So, surely, the first step to take in reducing greenhouse gas emissions from food production is to reduce waste?

Most of us are aware of global warming and we all have a view not always shared by people we know. It is, however, a global issue. The weather patterns and behaviour are interconnected and global. My country, the U.K., has aimed for zero emissions by 2030 or is it 2050 – it really makes no difference as there is no such thing as zero emissions.

Living organisms, humans and animals, emit gases merely by existing. And in any case, the 1.2% of global GGEs that the U.K. emits is relatively small amongst the developed nations of the world, although we are still in the top 20. Which means that most countries emit less than 1%. In my view it is more sensible to look at the world view and target the two main emitters of GGEs into the atmosphere:

1. The generation of energy from fossil fuel
2. The production of food.

The production of highly processed food, otherwise known as fast food, not only impacts upon the environment destroying CO_2 absorbing forests and farmland, but just as importantly, upon the health of its consumers, creating enormous pressures on health services and therefore eroding expenditure for other services.

INTO THE FUTURE

The New York times offered a tour of the world, post climate change, written by David Wallace- Wells.

I'm not sure when climate change ceases, if ever, but some of Wallace-Wells' observations are interesting.

There is a possibility that, due to more first-time animal encounters due to an increase in animal migrations, there could be more pandemics similar to Covid-19.

Every country will become hotter. European cities will heat up at a rate of 12 miles closer to the equator each year. Heatwaves will triple in frequency. However, some regions will experience monsoons creating green and verdant pastures where once there was desert.

Wildfires will become more common in Europe and London will see palm trees instead of oak trees, becoming more like Barcelona.

Animals will begin leaving their natural habitats migrating towards the poles. And 3 billion people may be forced to move – over a third of the total population, increasing political pressures on migration.

Richer nations will find ways of adapting, leaving poorer nations with greater problems and restrictions.

Oceans will grow 20% more acidic affecting fish stocks.

Oceans will rise by up to a metre and maybe much more.

If Greenland's icecap melted, sea levels would rise by 20 feet.

40% of agricultural land could experience drought by 2050, with the obvious casualties.

Huge numbers of people will experience bush fires, droughts, flooding, heat waves and food shortages frequently.

But much of this could be mitigated if only governments would act with greater urgency and collectively. Politics gets in the way. Countries do not join forces to cooperate but if they did, the heating of the planet would slow.

As 'natural' disasters such as fires, flooding, hurricanes, storms and droughts occur, many times more frequently, there will be far less time for recovery between these events so we have to imagine disasters like 'Hurricane Sandy' or Australia's 'Black Summer' occurring in the same place before full recovery is met, making it a risk to live there, which could lead to more migration. For many people, the new world will be a place of constant crisis.

We all know that the worst possible scenarios can be avoided, but NOT unless political divisions and ambitions can be overcome, which, sad to say, is unlikely. The technology is already with us to mitigate the worst possible outcomes but where governments are dependent upon the status quo, there will be little change, and here lies the problem.

Take food waste, as an example. Unless governments impose strict regulations backed by severe penalties, it will continue unabated. Additionally, unless alternative energy supplies are introduced with much greater urgency, the fossil fuel industry will continue to flourish, and our planet will continue to heat up. In short, a third of the world's population is heading rapidly towards catastrophic living conditions with disastrous consequences for all of us.

Chapter 17

Conclusion

Our body requires fuel and the fuel should be as free from toxins as possible, if we are to function normally. To function normally our pH must be between 7.35 and 7.45. In spite of the intricate mechanisms that regulate our pH level, highly acidic diets can alter our pH level with devastating effect.

The most influential foods are those which create an increase in acidity (acidosis). These can be found within the foods which are highly processed. Fast foods are highly processed. High in fats, salts, sugars but low in fibre and vitamins and minerals.

Acidosis affects the capacity of the body to generate energy. When the energy supply is affected, the mechanism for regulating our pH is compromised, enabling acidosis to persist.

When we feel fatigued, we tend to search for food to 'recharge our batteries', but if what we eat is acidic, as in fast food, we merely aggravate a bad position to a worse position.

When our body ceases to produce adequate energy, our immune system begins to falter and we become susceptible to toxic attack which can lead to illnesses ranging from a common cold to cancer.

It is entirely our own personal responsibility to take care of our body. It is, after all, our home during our time on this planet. Taking care of our body includes choosing our fuel (food), and if we choose contaminated fuel, our body will not function as it should. The first sign of this will be fatigue.

Many of us know very little about the things we consume other than the name, shape, colour and taste. And we know little about all the nutrients in our food apart from some popular notion that vegetables and fruit are good for us and fatty foods are not.

In earlier chapters I have made an attempt to draw attention to some of the nutrients in some foods and grouped them into simple categories of good, average and poor. On closer observation, should supermarkets be persuaded to mark every food item with one of the three categories? Very few shelves would be illuminated with 'good', which would prove that most supermarket food is either average or poor. By fuelling up on most packaged supermarket food, you are tending towards acidosis. This can, of course, be offset by choosing loose vegetables and fruits, which contain alkalines.

I hear a lot about how the pressures of work and raising a family reduce the amount of time available for cooking and, in some cases, even shopping. This presents the case for convenience foods, ready meals, food deliveries, takeaways and fast food deliveries. It is easier to pop into a fast food outlet than to roll up your sleeves, don an apron and start preparing a meal. We have become so accustomed to convenience food and have lost sight of home cooking and the joy of 'real' food. It is so much easier and more convenient to have someone else do the cooking, so we hand over control to others to provide the fuel that enables us to live. But what of the quality of the 'other' food? It is, speaking generally, of poor quality and will inevitably, if consumed regularly, lead to declining health. But the decline is very gradual. The symptoms are fatigue, stress, irritability, difficulty concentrating, weight gain, poor sleep, anxiety, reduced libido, itchy skin, constipation; perhaps you'd like to add to this list?

But that is just the start. Later in life, but earlier than expected, more serious problems arise.

Heart palpitations, stiffness in the joints, breathlessness, poor complexion, uncomfortable digestion pains – and we put these down to natural ageing: wear and tear.

And a few more years down the line, your first visit to the doctor for something much more serious and perhaps a small operation and a bag full of medications with their unpleasant side effects.

And all this is happening in a modern society of considerable wealth.

But along the way, you never suspect it is anything to do with the type of foods you have been consuming throughout your life. And why should you? All your friends bar a couple of vegans and the odd vegetarian have been eating the same way. Barbecues and lager. Takeaways. Pizza treats for the children. Out to the Italian for a pasta or the Indian for a curry; and how often do you cook a family meal full of fresh vegetables?

The fast food industry has dominated food production globally for generations. It drives farming methods, CAFOs, mass production for ever cheaper food, chemical intervention at the farm and in the processing. Genetic interference to aid transport and storage issues. Powerful political positioning concerning employment levels which are high. Huge turnover figures enabling vast funds to be used in advertising, marketing and presentation campaigns. Immense power, through lobbyists to influence government policy. The influence of the biggest food providers is global and growing, so the problems are not just at home on your high street, the problems are global, affecting people and environments everywhere, especially in emerging countries which will not be able to cope with the health issues they will face.

Like global warming, and as a participant in its cause, the fast-food industry is responsible not only for the quick fix pleasure of a quick fix snack, but for the slow grinding misery of a gradual decline in health and well-being.

It's naughty but nice while you sup with the devil.

It's just a little bit of sin to spice up life! It's almost Faustian!

But long-term addiction to fast food will, inevitably, lead to long-term misery as health deteriorates and life becomes intolerable. It's a slow death.

Chapter 1

[1] DNA. National Library of Medicine

[2] Sodium Pump. Pirahanchi, Y.; Jessa, R.; 'Physiology, Sodium-Potassium Pump' (2023)

[3] Putnam, R.; Cell Physiology Source Book (4th Ed. 2012) Acidosis. Introcellular pH regulation.

[4] Iodine fact sheet for health professionals. U.S. Dept. of Health and Human Sciences (2021)

[5] Gulichloo, I.; Gerriets, V.; 'Actions of anti-inflammatory drugs'. California North State University, College of Medicine (2023)

[6] Zimmerman, J.; McLaughlin, J.; 'Cellular Respiration'. Pediatric Critical Care (2011)

[7] Haddal, A.; Mohinddin, S.; 'Citric Acid Cycle'. Indiana University School of Medicine (2023)

[8] Kozlowskie, T.; Pallardy, S.; 'Krebs Cycle. Enzymes, Energetics and Respiration'. Physiology of Woody Plants (1997)

[9] Graham, J.; Traylor, J.; 'Cyanide'. Magnolia Regional Hospital. Health Centre, Grandview Hospital.

[10] Cutler, E. W.; 'Micro Miracles. Discover the healing power of enzymes.

[11] Dr. Hu and Associates. Study. (2014) JAMA International Medicine. (42.2% from Soda, energy/sports drinks) Journal of American Medical Association.

[12] (See (2) Sodium Pump.

Chapter 2

[13] Putnam, R.; 'Intracellular pH regulation'. Cell Physiology Source Book. (4th Edition, 2012).

[14] Sulphur in Food. Schmidt, K.; 'American Heart Association (03/2022).

[15] Ritz, E. et al; 'Phosphate Additivies in Food – A Health Risk'. Dtsch Arztebl Int. (2012) Published in Nat. Library of Medicine (2012).

[16] Watling, C.; 'Association between diet and cancer risk'. Cancer Epidemiology Unit for Oxford Population Health (2022).

[17] Trowel, H.; Burkitt, D.; 'Western Diseases: Their emergence and prevention'. Cambridge MA: Harvard University Press (1981).

Chapter 3

[18] Fraca, A. S.; Encyclopedia of Food Health (2016)

Chapter 4

[19] Biga, L. et al. 1st Edition. 'Protein Metabolism'. Open Education Resources. Oregon State University. Dept. of Anatomy and Physiology.

[20] Kendal, M. 'Ultra Processed Foods'. Optimising Nutrition (2022)

[21] Kalra. S. et al. Managing obese people with Type 2 Diabetes (2021)

[22] World Health Organisation. 'Eliminating tranfats in Europe' (2015)

[23] Ma, W. et al. 'Intake of dietary fibre ... and risk of diverticulitis'. American journal of gastroenterology (2019)

Chapter 6

[24] Cazolla, R. et al. Helyon 10.1016/j. helyon (2020) e05390 (Nov. 2020)

[25] Singh, M.; Chandorka, S. 'Food Chemistry'. Vol. 238 (2018) pps 117–124.

[26] Food Tables. Plaskett Nutritional Medicine College.

[27] Vitamin E and benefits. Rizvi, S. et al. Sultan Qaboos Medical Journal (2014)

[28] Hernandez, E. 'Functional Dietary Lipids' (2016)

[29] Colorado State University. B Vitamins. 'Water-Soluble-Vitamins: B-Complex and Vitamin C'.

[30] Yang, J.C. et al. 'Nutrients' (2023) – Biotine Deficiency – 15(2), 264; https://doi.org/10.3390/nu15020264

Chapter 7

[31] Lugasi, A. 'The role of antioxidants phytonutrients in the prevention of disease. Acta biologica szegediensis (2023)

[32] Healthline.com 'Evidence-based article on 'How cooking affects the nutrient content of foods'.

[33] Raka, D. 'The Elimination Diet'. Ch. 86. Integrative Medicine. 4th Edition. Elsevier, Inc. (2018)

[34] American Heart Foundation. 'Fish and Omega-3 fatty acids' (2022)

Chapter 8

[35] Geddes, D. T. 'Inside the lactating breast': J. Mid Women's Health 52(6): 556–63 (2007)

[36] Willett, W. C. et al. 'Milk and Health'. New England Journal of Medicine. 382; 7 (2020)

[37] Frassetto, L. et al. National Library of Medicine. Journal List. 'Nutrients'. (2018) doi: 10.3390/nu10040517.

[38] National Library of Medicine. BMJ (2015) 351: h4580.

[39] Journal of Cereal Science. Vol. 56. Issue 2. Pp 119–126 (2012)

[40] Bailey J., 'US per capita consumption of grains. 1970 and 2014' (2017)

[41] Wikipedia. Flour bleaching agents.

[42] Nuffield Dept. of Population Health (NDPH) 'Oxford Vegetarian Study'. (2020)

Chapter 9

[43] Alexander, H. '5 facts about acrylamide and cancer risk'. (2022) Anderson Cancer Center.

[44] Fukushima, Y. et al. 'Antioxidants'. (2009) For the American Chemical Society.

Chapter 10

[45] Ritchie, H.; Rosen, M. (2013) – 'Land Use'. Published online at OurWorldinData.org.

[46] Devon County Council.

Chapter 11

[47] McDonald, James and McBride (2009) "The transformation of O.S. livestock agriculture". Economic Information Bulletin.

[48] New York Natural Resources Defense Council. "Pollution from Giant Livestock Farms Threatens Public Health". Issue Areas: Water.

[49] Delgado, C. L. (2003) 'Rising rates of the consumption of meat and milk in developing countries has created a new food revolution.'

Chapter 12

[50] Gustavsson, J. Global food losses and food waste: Study conducted for the International Congress

"Save Food" at Interpack 2011, Dusseldorf. OCLC 112 6211917.

[51] United Nations Environment Programme (2021) Food Waste Index Report.

[52] Reuters (2013) from U.N. Report. Retrieved (2021)

[53] NRDC (2017) "New Report: Expiration Date Confusion Causing up to 90% of Americans to Waste Food".

[54] Huffington Post (2015) "6 billion pounds of perfectly edible produce is wasted every year because it's ugly."

[55] Tristam, S. (2009) Waste: Uncovering the Global Food Scandal: The True Cost of What the Global Food Industry Throws Away. Penguin. ISBN 978-0-14-103634-2.

[56] Parfit, J. et al (2010) "Food waste within food supply chains: quantification and potential for change to 2050."

[57] Gustavsson, J. et al (2011) Global Food Losses and Food Waste.

[58] Andrea, J. (2019) "More than half of all food production in Canada is lost or wasted, report says."

Chapter 13

[59] Marshall, Bonnie, M.; Levy, Stuart B. 'Food Animals and Antimicrobials: Impact on Human Health'.

Clinical Microbiology Reviews. 24(4): 717–733 (2011)

[60] Blaser, M. Missing Microbes (Henry Holt, 2014)

Chapter 14

[61] Extracts from article in 'Precision Nutrition.com'. Andrews, R. 'All about Genetically Modified Foods'.

[62] Plant Biotech News (2013) "The race towards the first genetically modified plant."

[63] Parson, G. (2012) "Opposition to Monsanto patent on Indian melons". The Hindu. Chennai. India

[64] Vidal, John (2000) "Biopirates who seek the greatest prizes." The Guardian.

[65] Bomey, N. "Big deal: Bayer getting Monsanto to $66 billion." USA Today.

[66] Clendennen, S. K., et al (1999) 'Genetic engineering of cantaloupe melons ....' Biology and Biochemistry of the plant hormone Ethylene II. Springer. Dordrecht.

Chapter 15

[67] Wikipedia. (McDonald's) (Yum) (Obesity)

Chapter 16

[68] Edgar – Food global emissions inventory of GHGs from food systems.

[69] Our World in Data: Environmental Impacts of Food Production.

[70] Food and Agricultural Organisation of the United Nations

www.ingramcontent.com/pod-product-compliance
Lightning Source LLC
Chambersburg PA
CBHW050358120526
44590CB00015B/1741